CREATIVE LIGHTING

CUSTOM AND DECORATIVE LUMINAIRES

Wanda Jankowski

 PBC INTERNATIONAL, INC.

Distributor to the book trade in the United States and Canada
Rizzoli International Publications
through St. Martin's Press
175 Fifth Avenue
New York, NY 10010

Distributor to the art trade in the United States and Canada
PBC International, Inc.
One School Street
Glen Cove, NY 11542

Distributor throughout the rest of the world
Hearst Books International
1350 Avenue of the Americas
New York, NY 10019

Library of Congress Cataloging–in–Publication Data
Jankowski, Wanda.
Creative lighting: custom and decorative luminaires / by Wanda Jankowski.
    p.   cm.
  Includes indexes.
    ISBN 0–86636–343–2 (hb)   ISBN 0–86636–547–8 (pb)
    1. Lighting, architectural and decorative.   I. Title
NK2115.5.L5J345   1997
729'.28—dc20   CIP
                                                    97–19297

CAVEAT– Information in this text is believed accurate, and will pose no
problem for the student or casual reader. However, the author was often
constrained by information contained in signed release forms, information
that could have been in error or not included at all. Any misinformation
(or lack of information) is the result of failure in these attestations. The
author has done whatever is possible to insure accuracy.

Color separation Fine Arts Repro House, Hong Kong
Printing and binding by South China Printing Co. (1988) Ltd., H.K.

10 9 8 7 6 5 4 3 2 1

Printed in Hong Kong

*To Claudia, Roger,
Michael, Christine. . .
and Sheba, some of
the most important
lights in my life.*

CONTENTS

CREATIVE LIGHTING

CUSTOM AND DECORATIVE LUMINAIRES

"Through the art of lighting, the composition of the spaces or places we occupy or pass through is revealed."

FOREWORD

Light is a word that evokes a wide range of feelings within different people. To a philosopher, it is the metaphor of knowledge, to a scientist it is a fundamental component of his work, and to the scenic artist it is a tool to manipulate emotion. To the rest of us, it is the primary medium by which we acquire information. But what is light? Light is visually radiant energy—the trigger of our perceptions.

Light is one of the most malleable of all design tools. Through the art of lighting, the composition of the spaces or places we occupy or pass through is revealed. It is difficult to imagine a man-made space today that would not have some lighting as a part of the scheme.

Fine lighting is achieved through careful consideration of two questions: "What goals have been set for this design?" and "How can the success of the system in achieving those goals be measured?" Good lighting must be defined at the start of every project with each client. Since light is visually evaluated and creates perceptions, numbers methodology cannot fulfill the expectations that abound with every new project. Instead, a clear description of what will make good lighting should be recorded prior to the beginning of the design.

Today, the contribution that lighting has made to architecture and interior design is clearly recognizable and made most evident by the use of lighting designers as collaborators with architects and interior designers, and by the growth of lighting design as a profession. The pages of this book contain examples of projects in which carefully prepared lighting designs are evident. The achievements of the examples that follow are as clear as the medium itself.

Howard M. Brandston,
FIES, FCIBSE, FIALD
Principal, H.M. Brandston & Partners, Inc.

PREFACE

"...if we study the 1920s and 1930s, we can find a glimpse of the seeds of today's artistic flourish."

The history of architectural ornament is part of the history of humans building—from the Egyptian temples on the Nile, the Greek and Roman monuments, the Gothic cathedrals, the Renaissance palaces to America's great skyscrapers of today. In each era, with the exception of the austerity and bare simplicity found in post-war periods, artists and craftsmen have lent their skills and talent to the adornment and enhancement of doors, windows, fireplaces, cornices, columns, and other locations where enrichment is called for and logical. Some of the most important elements in the history of building have been the devices humans have created for generating artificial lighting.

All artificial illumination was generated by flame until 1879, when Thomas Edison solved the riddle of the electric light. Since then, we have gradually come to grips with the great possibilities of the age of light without flame. With initial trepidation, we began using electric light in our buildings. We hesitantly substituted weak, bare carbon filament lamps for the flames which had been in gaslights, or in architectural elements such as capitals and arches.

The switch to electricity gradually became more simple as invention flourished. Thomas Edison created some of the most original fixtures during this period, such as the great chandelier in the Assembly in the New Jersey State House in Trenton, or his beautiful pendant fixture in St. Paul's United Methodist Church near his hometown in Tiffin, Ohio.

The tungsten filament arrived in the marketplace in 1904 and sparked the true evolution of lighting. The light output increased three or four times the approximate intensity of a gas flame. The masterpieces of the art metal craftsmen and creative reproductions of Renaissance ornament which used the original low-wattage carbon filament lamps, became platforms for overly bright lamps in the 1920s and 1930s. These beautiful bronze and wrought iron fixtures became glaring suns which overwhelmed the architectural environment, as demand for higher light levels grew.

Advances in lamp technology have driven the evolution of the lighting fixture. Early efforts in the Art Deco and Art Moderne periods of the 1920s and 1930s to control light with reflectors for indirect lighting blossomed in the 1950s and 1960s. Lamps became smaller. Optically designed reflectors achieved better control of the light, and today we approach the ideal—the ability to deliver given light intensities to proscribed surfaces without the source creating irritating glare.

In the 1970s and 1980s, decorative fixtures did not necessarily have to hold the principal sources of illumination in a building. Engineered lighting equipment generated the necessary functional light, be it task/reading light or accent/theatrical spotlights hidden in architectural elements. The pendant chandeliers, wall sconces, and interior standards again became independent artworks. The fixture designer studied the architectural spirit of a building, caught the character and personality of that individual courthouse, library, or church, crystallized the design motif and reflected it, bringing it to its clearest statement without concern for primary lighting. Today, the ornamental arts are flourishing again as they have through the ages.

Indeed, artists and craftsmen are creating pieces that enhance a building. The present lament of architects that there are no craftsmen left in America, is disproved by this collection of case studies and examples of luminaires. They are alive and well and at work wherever they are asked, performing with a great burst of original design and technique.

Of course, if we study the 1920s and 1930s, we can find a glimpse of the seeds of today's artistic flourish. America's first lighting consultant, Louis B. Marks, for example, used decorative fixtures beautifully.

Moreover, the fixtures of each period stylistically took on the architectural character of that era. The Victorian fixtures were exuberant; the Beaux Arts fixtures classic; the Art Nouveau fixtures sensuous; the Bauhaus fixtures disciplined, strict and severe. Today's fixtures display a great love of the richness of material, and a desire to create a flourish. Architects frame a doorway with a pair of brackets or hang a chandelier in a lobby with the same suggestion of elegance that a simple string of pearls or a spectacular diamond brooch give to fashion.

As decorative fixtures are again coming into their own, light levels are dropping and interest in historic restoration is increasing. Both these forces affect our subject. The energy crisis, and subsequent need to conserve fuel, has resulted in a national energy code that calls for lower light levels. The interest in preserving the great buildings of the past has resulted in a deeper appreciation and understanding of the architectural styles and ornamental arts of our forefathers. We have also slowed the destruction of old buildings and have gained respect for the craftsmanship in our built environment.

All these forces have come together during our time and generation, and Wanda Jankowski has caught the spirit of our age. Having lived and worked in the lighting field for her adult life, she knows and understands current lighting trends and tells us about it in detail with a comprehension only her love of it could portray. Enjoy the discoveries her illuminations reveal.

Viggo Bech Rambusch, FIES, ASID
Chairman, Rambusch Decorating Company

INTRODUCTION

"This book explores how decorative luminaires are currently used in major installations including restaurants, offices, building lobbies, schools, hotels, and retail establishments."

As times change, fashion pendulums swing and sensibilities that gain favor in one era fall into disfavor and are replaced in another. The infant lighting industry was affected by developments in technology in the 1960s and 1970s. Vast arrays of ceiling troffers and recessed downlights became commonplace because, at the time, they were thought to be sophisticated and modern. The streamlined look was state-of-the-art, and energy saving was not a major concern.

Today, technology has brought many refinements to lighting. Complex, but bulky components in fixtures have been replaced with electronic era packages that are smaller in size. Compact and more varied types of light sources have allowed smaller fixture housings to be developed. Energy efficiency and lumen outputs have improved and more sophisticated controls have increased the versatility of lighting systems. Electronic ballasts have virtually replaced electro-magnetic models.

Advanced technologies have permeated most aspects of all our lives, as well as the lighting industry. Computers and fax machines are becoming as common as the tele-

phone. Yet, the human reaction to high-tech is one of ambivalence. Check the results of any consumer survey and invariably it will indicate that as much as consumers marvel at and desire the conveniences offered by the latest electronic wonders, they also yearn for back-to-basics products—from healthier, more natural foods, to more casual and comfortable clothing styles made of natural fibers.

This pendulum swing to a middle ground in which the benefits of technology coexist with comforts drawn from nature is reflected in the lighting industry. Today, consumers express an increased interest in decorative luminaires, both as the primary lighting system, and in combination with architectural, recessed lighting elements.

Currently, there are more types of interesting materials available for use in decorative luminaires than ever before—from treated papers and textured glass, to wire mesh and faux-painted acrylics. Decorative luminaires can bring a large volume area or building exterior down to human scale, and warmly enrich a space through glowing, colorful, and tactile materials.

There is increased interest in preserving the past by restoring the beauty of historic buildings and interiors. Decorative fixtures often play a significant role in establishing the character of these environments, whether they are office buildings, houses of worship, banks, government agencies, schools or hotels.

Technology is improving the variety and quality of lighting effects achievable. Yet many architects and designers must seek solutions to lighting spaces that may be technically simple, but need to exhibit a highly developed sense of color, form and texture, and a refined understanding of the relationship of light to objects and surfaces in space.

In order to remain competitive in today's highly developed marketplace, clients increasingly demand something special from lighting professionals. This translates into an increased demand for custom-designed luminaires to fully express the architect's or designer's vision for the space. Options to suit the budget range from completely custom luminaires to combination fixtures that blend off-the-shelf elements with custom components.

This book explores how decorative luminaires are currently used in major installations, including restaurants, offices, building lobbies, schools, hotels, and retail establishments. A range of luminaires are also detailed—from standard fixtures to custom design, and everything in between. Care has been taken to include an array of fixture and interior styles, from historic restorations and classical chandelier designs, to eclectic combinations and streamlined, contemporary elements.

An extensive product section is incorporated to provide the reader with insight into the wealth of creative talent available in the production of decorative luminaires. Products are included from major manufacturers of both custom and standard products in traditional as well as contemporary stylings, and from smaller companies and individual artisans who specialize in a particular blending of materials or who express a singular vision. A concerted effort has been made to showcase luminaires that run the gamut in variety of materials. Unusual paint finishes, textured glass, acrylic, varied metals, treated papers, wire mesh and even ostrich eggs have been explored as suitable for use in decorative luminaires.

The Americans with Disabilities Act (ADA) affected many design elements, including lighting. The act requires that lighting fixtures mounted between 27 inches and 80 inches high on walls in public-access areas not project more than 4 inches from the wall. Many manufacturers have been quick to respond to this government mandate with fixture lines that are both functional and beautiful. Examples of ADA compliant luminaires in a variety of styles are included in the product section of this book.

My gratitude and appreciation extends to everyone who has contributed their knowledge and expertise to this book.

Wanda Jankowski

CREATIVE
LIGHTING

RESTAURANT INTERIORS

SPOT BAGEL BAKERY NEWMARK

The owner of Spot Bagel Bakery Newmark held a design competition to create a prototype image for the store, inviting five firms to do schematic designs for a stipend. The owner had established a strong corporate identity through graphics, logo and an aggressive marketing campaign, and had in mind to raise the humble and modest product to a new level by creating a kind of "bagel theater" experience for his customers.

Adams/Mohler Architects entered the competition and created the winning design for the 1,400-square-foot space. Keeping extraneous elements to a minimum, the architects have combined extremes, mixing the prehistoric with the futuristic. According to Rik Adams, "It's a kind of Fred Flintstone meets George Jetson atmosphere."

The architects were aware of the owner's love of lava lamps, and so incorporated them into the lighting scheme. They custom created a light fixture using modified lava lamps, adding

brackets and a shade over halogen PAR lamps, and suspending it. Wire is concealed in flowing lines of flexible metal conduit.

Bare Circline fluorescent lamps are also used as decorative elements, and like parts of a spaceship, surround the central column and swirls of ceiling-mounted sheet metal that mimic the bagel's circular shape.

The central column is illuminated with 6-foot fluorescent tubes concealed behind the galvanized sheet metal. Tables clustered around it add to the nightclub quality of the space.

Additional illumination over the counters and in the sales area are provided by recessed compact fluorescent downlights.

The walls and floor embody prehistoric elements. Cryptic murals have been handpainted by local artists. The flooring is original concrete treated with a pigmented sealer.

Adams/Mohler Architects received an Honor Award from the Seattle Chapter of the American Institute of Architects (AIA) and a Northwest Pacific Regional AIA Award for this project.

above The custom fixture includes a lava lamp positioned above a shade that houses a halogen PAR lamp.
opposite The wall murals are handpainted, and the concrete flooring is treated with a pigmented sealer.

LOCATION: Seattle, Washington ARCHITECTS & LIGHTING DESIGNERS: Rik Adams and Rick Mohler, Adams/Mohler Architects DESIGN CONSULTANTS: Eclectic Surfaces, Patti Swenson Perbix CONTRACTOR: Krekow Jennings Inc. PHOTOGRAPHER: Robert Pisano LIGHTING MANUFACTURERS: Lightolier, Lava Simplex Internationale

left Fluorescent Circline lamps are used as decorative elements and work with the swirling sheet metal to create a futuristic atmosphere.

BAANG

Baang is a Chinese word that means "to bind or tie together," and was selected as the name for this family-style, Greenwich, Connecticut restaurant to reflect the blending of French and Asian cuisine, and whimsy combined with elements of Asian design. The modest stucco exterior has been designed to intentionally create the impression that the diner is about to enter a traditional Connecticut structure—even included are authentic Woolworth revolving doors that lead into the 4,500-square-foot space.

The contemporary interior reflects the notion of "fusion" by blending subtle tones and hues, and avoiding primary colors. Exotic spices from New York's Chinatown were purchased and studied in order to create the ginger-root yellow, chili-pepper red, and leek green tones of the walls and floor. This subtle color scheme is revealed as well in the oxidized handcrafted copper railing that runs along the wooden platform elevating the bar and a large portion of the dining room. Colored discs have been scattered within the railing to evoke a sense of playfulness.

The high-ceilinged room includes the kitchen, dining room, and bar area. In addition to a custom-designed sofa and grand banquette, striking elements of the space include four oxidized copper poles. Copper mesh clouds, approximately 18 feet long, sit atop the poles and have been inspired by Asian pagodas and copper woks. The columns contain spotlights at two levels that cast light up toward the ceiling.

The bar area includes persimmon-colored loveseats, a curvacious zinc-topped bar, and glass shelving contained in a circular display element illuminated with concealed low-voltage striplights. Pendant fixtures, imported from France and designed by Jean Michel Labrat, are made with stiffened nylon material and house simple A-lamps. Decorative fixtures, which add texture to the effect of the space, are complemented by track lighting elements used in the dining area.

above Two levels of uplight come from the four columns scattered throughout the interior.
opposite Hanging fixtures made from nylon material are fitted with A-lamps.

LOCATION: **Greenwich, Connecticut** OWNER: **Jody Pennette** LIGHTING AND INTERIOR DESIGNER: **David Rockwell, Rockwell Group**
PHOTOGRAPHER: **©Paul Warchol** LIGHTING MANUFACTURERS: **Detournement De Coulers, Lucifer Lighting**

Spices from New York's Chinatown were studied to produce the ginger-root yellow, chili-pepper red, and leek green tones of the walls and floor.

CORNERSTONE GRILL

The building that now houses the 10,000-square-foot Cornerstone Grill had previously contained a restaurant. However, the new owner wanted to create a space that emphasized the lounge and nightclub aspects of the dining and entertainment establishment, so patrons could enjoy the half-dozen or so billiard tables available as well.

The existing space, reminiscent of New Orleans architecture, contained some unusual features, including brickwork arches, and fully operational gaslight sconces. The design team combined the nostalgic elements of times past with custom-made contemporary metalwork, flooring and furnishings.

The lighting fixtures have been custom designed so that they are fully tailored to the space. Some of the luminaires have glass diffusers, and others have acrylic lenses. Many are detailed with swirls of metal that add vibrancy to gently glowing pendant bowls. Fixtures are lamped with incandescent sources, primarily A-lamps and MR 16s.

All these lighting fixtures are controlled by a computerized dimming system so varied scenes can be created throughout the day to suit different functions.

Tactile surfaces are used to clearly define space changes (the restaurant exceeds all ADA requirements as well). And varied textures and colors are used to enrich the sensory experience of the space. Velvet draperies and harlequin booth fabric play against the ornate tin ceiling, brickwork and metal railings. Occasional accents of bright red upholstery or floor tiles are counterpoints to the dark wood grains of the counters and furnishings. Even the gas sconces have been embellished with beads and chain mail.

above Juxtaposition of varied tactile elements adds vibrancy to the space. ***left*** The beauty of the luminaries is evident by day as well as by night. ***opposite*** The entry pendant combines bowl and cone elements used separately in fixtures in other areas of the restaurant.

LOCATION: **Brea, California** OWNER: **Craig Hofman** INTERIOR DESIGNER: **Hatch Design Group** PHOTOGRAPHER: **Cameron Carothers** LIGHTING MANUFACTURERS: **Morrison Lighting**

above Harlequin booth fabric and brilliant red floor and wall coverings play against the rough-textured brickwork.
left The brickwork, ornate tin ceiling, and operational gas sconces were original to the space.

above All the fixtures have been custom fabricated for maximum integration into the design of the space.

left Irregularly placed luminaires add to the drama and surprise of the space.

opposite Cornerstone Grill is not only a destination for dining, but for nightclubbing and billiards as well. Lighting helps to set a "stage" that envelops the guest.

GLOUCESTER RESTAURANT

"It's sort of like Rockefeller Center meets 1927 New York jazz," says interior designer, Charles Morris Mount, of the Gloucester restaurant, formerly the Gloucester House seafood restaurant. The new owner gave the designer a free hand in deciding how to express a fantastical combination of Baroque and Art Deco in the 7,500 square feet of space.

The 300-seat restaurant is located in a midtown-Manhattan, three-story Art Moderne/Deco structure built in 1927.

The interior is filled with rich layer upon layer of imagery and detail. The 5,000-square-foot main floor is entered through mahogany and bevelled glass French doors. Not to be missed are three large, custom handcrafted coiled copper and glass chandeliers suspended from the 19-foot-high ceiling. The main chandelier is 8 feet in diameter; the remaining two are 7 feet wide. The sunburst motif in the grand chandeliers is repeated in the mural panels and colorful floor tiles. The ceiling's painted abstract of New York skyscrapers forming a sunburst were painted at a New York artist's studio and applied at the site.

The visual feast in the main dining area also includes a wealth of varied furnishings, materials and displays. There are musical themes reflecting 1930s jazz, such as the black and white piano key design on tabletops. Wall murals depict the classical mythological characters of Apollo and Diana.

Seating includes custom-designed in-laid tables, woven chairs and upholstered booths. In the center of the floor, a custom display table made of copper, glass, marble and in-laid wood surrounds a refrigerated produce/seafood case. At the rear of the main floor there is a maple and stainless steel display kitchen with pizza oven.

The 2,500-square-foot mezzanine is reached via a grand staircase punctuated by a series of custom torchieres that also adorn the mezzanine railing at regular intervals. The luminaires are made with copper and resin set aglow by concealed bands of neon in three shades of blue beginning with the darkest at the bottom and lightening gradually upward.

The mezzanine contains a rectangular bar with a row of television screens along one

above Torchieres are set at regular intervals on the railing of the 2,500-square-foot mezzanine. **opposite** Grand chandeliers designed by Jim Welty are suspended from the 19-foot-high ceiling of the main dining hall.

LOCATION: New York City OWNERS: Peter Skeadas, Louis Pappas and John Karayiannis LIGHTING AND INTERIOR DESIGNER: Charles Morris Mount, Charles Morris Mount Inc. ARCHITECT: Costas Terzis GRAPHIC DESIGNER: Ine Wijtvliet, Wijtvliet Design MURALIST: Michael Cotten CHANDELIER DESIGNER: James Welty, Autre Monde Artifacts NEON AND TORCHIERE DESIGNER: Terry Thompson Lighting Design Fabricators CONTRACTOR: Bristol Construction PHOTOGRAPHER: Norman McGrath LIGHTING MANUFACTURER: Lightolier—pendants at bar

wall. Patrons can use individual earphones located at each set to listen to programs on the channel of their choice. The wall is highlighted by frosted glass panels backlit with neon. The mezzanine also contains tables and chairs, as well as

booths, surrounded by walls adorned with bevelled mirrors.

Decorative luminaires are supplemented by recessed MR 16 downlights that provide task and ambient illumination.

above Repeated motifs include piano key patterns,
sunbursts and classical mythological figures.

above Stairway torchieres are illuminated with varied shades of blue neon.

left In addition to custom-designed luminaires, recessed MR 16 downlights provide "enough light to read a newspaper by."

This particular Cheesecake Factory—part of an ever-expanding chain in the U.S.—is located in the White Flint mall in suburban Bethesda, Maryland. In addition to the 40 flavors of cheesecake available in this full-service, 9,000-square-foot facility, are approximately 200 other moderate-priced food items.

The space used for the Cheesecake Factory had previously housed five retail stores. One of the major challenges for Hatch Design Group, the design firm for the Cheesecake Factory, had been to adapt the restaurant chain's design elements to this irregular-shaped space, and to give the establishment a striking enough exterior identity to attract patrons easily in the busy mall.

The 140-foot-long exterior is punctuated by a classical Roman facade entrance that playfully mimics the classical federal buildings that proliferate in nearby Washington, D.C. Indentations, curves and windows using cherry veneer, copper and granite create visual interest in the remaining 120 feet of the exterior.

The restaurant interior is eclectic and blends several

left Luscious desserts are accented with light cast from decorative luminaires suspended above. Forty flavors of cheesecake are available to patrons.

styles, including Victorian, French, Art Deco and Egyptian. Traditional elements, such as rich woods are juxtaposed with contemporary steel accents. Decorations and patterns abound—in the limestone floors, the faux-finished ceilings and walls, and the decorative ceiling murals. Diners are afforded privacy via elegant etched glass dividers.

The sconces and decorative pendants reflect the eclecticism of the other furnishings. All are custom made with glass dif-

fusers in a variety of styles. Most are lamped with incandescent A-lamps.

In addition to the array of decorative luminaires, unobtrusive architectural lighting systems provide both accent and general illumination. Rows of downlights highlight traffic patterns. Low-voltage halogen strip-lights tucked into painted plaster columns uplight Egyptian-style leaves mounted on the column tops. Concealed light strips illuminate painted ceiling coves.

LOCATION: **Bethesda, Maryland** OWNER: **David Overton** INTERIOR DESIGN AND LIGHTING FIRM: **Hatch Design Group**
PHOTOGRAPHER: **Kenneth Wyner** LIGHTING MANUFACTURER: **Morrison Lighting**

above All the decorative luminaires in The Cheesecake Factory are custom made. Downlights illuminate traffic patterns.

far left Ceiling-mounted decorative fixtures highlight the bar area. The eclectic decor combines French, Victorian, Art Deco and Egyptian styles.

left A custom chandelier draws diners' attention to the maitre d' station.

COCO LOCO RESTAURANT

Under the overall thematic umbrella of Brazilian styling, Adamstein & Demetriou Architects have juxtaposed neoclassical, baroque, Portuguese, tropical and modern design elements in Coco Loco Restaurant. A sidewalk cafe atmosphere is created immediately upon entry. Potted palms, Spanish tile floors, wicker chairs and Rebecca Cross custom painted tabletops depicting tropical fruit and greenery, bring the flavor of the tropical Brazilian rain forests to Washington, D.C. The front space also contains a 9-foot by 9-foot painting by Lenore Winters capturing fruit pickers on a sultry afternoon in Brazil. Ceramic mosaics in contemporary designs executed by Tom Ashcraft frame the main dining level, where an open kitchen and rotisserie hearth are located. A colorful bar is positioned beneath a rich, red canopy that echoes the horns of a Spanish bull. The center of the restau-

rant is distinguished by six columns, each in a different color. An adjacent dining area can be transformed into a dance floor and stage area for live performances of Latin music or flamenco dancing. The beauty of the area is heightened by a 14-foot by 11-foot painting by Raimundo Rubio of Anton Gallery. Juxtaposed with a clean, recessed downlighting scheme that casts gentle pools of light over tables and in the bar area are custom designed decorative fixtures. The back dining area contains an array of custom fixtures by A&D, fabricated

by Robert Lewis of Haywire. These 10-foot-long bamboo pods are evocative of primitive Amazon imagery. Elongated vertical bamboo lights and hanging rounded fixtures are interspersed in other areas of the restaurant.

above Earthy colors are used in the furnishings and light fixtures to evoke a tropical atmosphere.
opposite The red canopy over the bar area is stylized reminiscence of the horns of a Spanish bull.

LOCATION: **Washington, D.C.** OWNER: **Savino Recine and Yannick Cam** ARCHITECT AND INTERIOR DESIGNER: **Adamstein & Demetriou Architects** ARCHITECT OF RECORD: **Russell Sears** ELECTRICAL CONTRACTOR: **Spectrum Electric** PHOTOGRAPHER: **Maxwell Mackenzie** LIGHTING MANUFACTURERS: **Robert Lewis of Haywire**

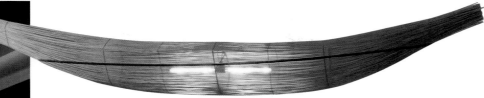

left The bamboo fixtures are combined in a variety of shapes and sizes and complement the colors of the six columns in the dining area.

below The lightng fixtures include these 10-foot-long suspended pods made of bamboo.

The Water Grill is a sophisticated supper club in Los Angeles, California. It combines classical lines with streamlined moderne design and some 1990s twists. As guests walk past the swag of royal purple velvet at the entryway, a rich color scheme incorporating hues of purple, teal and golden ochre is revealed in the floor tiles and furnishings.

A rich blending of unusual materials characterizes the club. The bar is anegré wood and zinc. The lounge area at the front of the restaurant is paneled with a golden colored wood and combined with furnishings upholstered in gold and purple.

The bar is separated from the dining area by curvilinear wall details and ribbed glass windows. The dining room, adorned in teal and gold, heavily woven fabrics and carpet, is distinguished by high paneled private booths.

Decorative luminaires include pendants formed with curved sheets of slumped glass and patina brass, created by Pam Morris. These are lamped with low-voltage light sources for a clean, white look. Multi-stemmed glass pendants by Neidhardt are attached to the glass and wood display shelves above the bar. These luminaires are intended to represent abstractions of fanciful fish. The aquatic theme is carried through in wall murals depicting Los Angeles landmarks whimsically set among caricatures of the sea.

Architectural lighting elements are used as well to provide accent and ambient illumination. For example, recessed downlights illuminate the dining area, and track units highlight artwork on the walls.

above Pendants add visual interest and a warm glow to the entry corridor.

LOCATION: **Los Angeles, California** OWNER: **University Restaurant Group** INTERIOR DESIGN FIRM: **Hatch Design Group** ELECTRICAL CONTRACTOR: **Rowe Electric** LIGHT ARTIST: **Pam Morris Designs: Exciting Lighting** PHOTOGRAPHER: **Martin Fine** LIGHTING MANUFACTURER: **Neidhardt**

above   Pools of light are cast on the zinc bar
countertop by the low-voltage sconces.
left   Objects displayed on the glass shelves are
highlighted by recessed lights.

above Curved, slumped glass fixtures have been custom created by Pam Morris for the space.

right The Water Grill combines classic lines with more streamlined moderne design.

above Hues of teal, purple and golden ochre are used throughout the supper club. The aquatic theme appears in the wall murals.
left Delicate sconces of metal and glass are like abstract fish.
opposite Track units accent artwork and floral arrangements.

"It's not just about screwing light bulbs in the ceiling," says artist and designer Pam Morris. Her luminaire creations are a direct outgrowth of her philosophies about light. With the discovery of electric light, light has become our "functional slave," explains Morris, allowing us to work at night wherever we prefer. At the same time, this development deprives us of the primitive gatherings around the campfire that afforded the opportunity to tell stories, create myths, and grow closer to each other from the shared, human fears of the dark and the unknown.

Working with light for Morris also means working with energy, forces and power. It is logical then, given such a kinetic medium, that people should feel and react to her creations, to receive the energy and power with their bodies, so that experiencing the lighting is both physical and emotional.

An interesting point Morris makes is that in centuries past, people knew how houses were made, and how cloth was woven, because it was done all by them and by hand. But most of us today do not know how

left Attention to detail in Chops Atlanta extends to the design and construction of the custom table lamps, masterpieces of color, texture and form.

the fax machine or the computer is really made. And this lack of knowledge has made us feel insecure and inadequate, despite a surface veneer of sophistication. Visceral, textural luminaires are one way to put a human footprint on the experience of the environment. It's a sign that a human made it; it's Pam Morris saying, "Here, this is for you."

"Customers are not only buying food and service, they're buying a sensory experience as well, and if the environment is visually rich, they will feel they're getting their money's worth," says Morris. "The difference between a $200 per square foot space and a $300 per square foot budget is in the millwork, lighting, and special details. Chops Atlanta is an example of a project where the market reality proved correct. Without the millwork, custom lighting, and special details, it would have been rather ordinary. It would never have the

LOCATION: **Atlanta, Georgia**   INTERIOR DESIGNER: **Pat Culeto, Culeto Consulting and Design**   LIGHTING DESIGNER: **Pam Morris Designs: Exciting Lighting**   CONTRACTOR: **W.P. Tatum Co.**   PHOTOGRAPHER: **Alan McGee**

Geometrically shaped custom luminaires of metal and glass complement the richly detailed, traditional-styled interior of Chops Atlanta.

visual richness and sense of quality that established customers' trust."

The angular fixtures over the bar in Chops Atlanta are made of nickel-plated, formed bronze and cast glass. The chandeliers are made with Austrian crystal and forged iron.

LONGSHOREMAN'S DAUGHTER

The owner of an existing business—an espresso shop—wanted to open a restaurant that, according to Adams/Mohler Architects, "would evoke the spirit of the Northwest Longshore while revealing the underlying formal structure of the space."

Brent Markee, a local artist, custom designed three pendant luminaires for the dining area. Each fixture is spun brass with an ebonized finish. Resting in the metal bowl are three MR 16s, each aimed upward at a yellowish disc mounted to the ceiling. The discs, made of medium-density fiberboard, are elliptical, as is the path of light that emanates from the pendant and shines upon it.

"Schoolhouse" fixtures, with opaque glass globes, are suspended over a counter. The architects found the fixtures, and added rods and connectors. Quilted stainless steel on a back wall behind these fixtures gives the space a touch of a 1950s diner look.

Most striking are the images

of the longshore evoked by the wall murals, handpainted by local artists. "The walls contain text and images taken directly from the Port of Tacoma (where the owner's father was, in fact, a longshoreman)," says Rik Adams. He notes that longshoremen who happen to come to the restaurant recognize some of the numbers used on the walls, which have genuine meaning for them.

Metal is used throughout the space, reminiscent of sailing and docked ships. Decorative steel plate clads the columns and the bar.

Rick Mohler and Rik Adams say the roles they played on this project were more as directors than as the typical lead architects of a design team. The owner and architects collaborated with a small army of local artists and craftsmen, each of whom contributed talent and ideas to make the final outcome a success.

above Schoolhouse fixtures and a wall of quilted stainless steel are reminiscent of a 1950s-style diner.
opposite In the bowl of the pendant are three MR 16s which cast light up to the fiberboard discs.

LOCATION: **Seattle, Washington** OWNER: **Lori Lynn Mason** ARCHITECTS & INTERIOR DESIGNERS: **Rik Adams and Rick Mohler, Adams/Mohler Architects** LIGHTING AND DESIGN CONSULTANTS: **Brent Markee, Eclectic Surfaces, David Gulassa**
PHOTOGRAPHER: **Robert Pisano**

right The longshore is evoked particularly in the images of the wall murals, and in the use of decorative steel plate on the columns and bar.

Each restaurant in the Louise's Trattoria chain is designed specifically to complement its site location. The freestanding building chosen for Louise's in Brentwood had been used as a restaurant with a Western motif and menu. But before the renovation could begin, the architects and designers had to meet requirements and review by the local community board. In addition, this Louise's faced intense competition from the numerous eating establishments already existing throughout the San Vincente Scenic Corridor area.

The facade of the restaurant has been redesigned to resemble an Italianate church and pulled back about 15 feet from the street to create a two-level plaza. The upper plaza is surrounded by plantings and a fountain.

The building itself is canted toward a large public clock on the corner of the street.

The interior of the previous restaurant had been cavelike, with uncomfortable, abrupt transitions in lighting from too bright to too dark. The goal for Louise's was to make the two-level interior as open and pleas-

ant as possible. This is accomplished by combining decorative and architectural lighting elements.

Easily noticed are the delicate decorative fixtures in varied styles placed throughout the spaces. There is a row of pendants with small, Murano glass circular diffusers, and circular wall sconces, as well as a large Artichoke fixture that is lamped with 500-watt A-type lamps.

These elements are comple-

mented by underlit glass shelves, skylights and beam-mounted track fixtures. Though the sunlight from them is enjoyed by patrons during the day, the skylights are not immediately noticeable because they are tapered. At roofline, they measure about 2 feet by 8 feet. At the interior ceiling line, they are approximately 3½ feet by 8 feet. In evening hours, fixtures mounted on the roof outside the skylights provide illumination to

above The facade resembles an Italianate church. The umbrellas are underlit with low-voltage strings of lights.

LOCATION: **Brentwood, California**   ARCHITECTS & INTERIOR DESIGNERS: **Peter C. Merwin and James Weiner Architect**   CONTRACTOR: **Dan Barling, Woodward and Sprowl**   ELECTRICAL ENGINEER: **Amelect**   PHOTOGRAPHER: **Tom Bonner**   LIGHTING MANUFACTURERS: **Leucos, Poulsen, Flos, Halo, Capri, Stonco, Lucifer, Lumiere, Hubbell, Surelite, and Alkco**

left Pendants and sconces supplement the array of track fixtures.
below Skylights and sconces blend to create a comfortable, open and airy ambiance in the room.

Track fixtures mounted on ceiling beams illuminate the high, vaulted ceiling. The decorative Artichoke fixture is lit with A-lamps.

the interior. The double-dome, diffused skylights are cleaned regularly to maintain a high-quality level of illumination.

To keep the ceiling plane free of overt fixtures, track units are mounted on the beams and provide uplighting of the ceiling above, and highlighting of elements below.

The kitchen in the deli/bar area is illuminated with track lights tucked into the soffit for a soft, indirect approach. Glass stems sparkle from the backlighting of the glass rack with 4-foot-long fixtures. The upper dining area has a pool of light focused on each table. This project conforms with Title 24 energy codes, and uses energy efficiently at the tabletops. Trafficways are illuminated largely with spill light.

Though each Louise's is site-specific, the way the light is used remains the same from one location to the next, even though the fixtures used to achieve it change, thus maintaining a consistent ambiance throughout the chain.

 GRANITA

The concept for Granita, set by interior designer Barbara Lazaroff, involved creating a sense of the variation and complexity of an underwater grotto. Pam Morris' blown glass sculptures, that are often combined with patinated metals and inset crystals, are abstract interpretations of magical sea creatures. Most of the fixtures use MR 16, MR 11 or PAR 20 lamps. Exterior and interior columns are topped with ivory bubble collars and enveloped with verdigris copper forms that resemble sea kelp.

Wall washers and adjustable "eyeball" fixtures are positioned to illuminate artwork and architectural elements, such as curving soffits, the reception desk, and stone design on the wood-burning oven.

Morris believes she is not working with glass, but rather working with light, using a variety of materials to transport it. And because glass needs to be supported, she will combine it with whatever metal best suits the character of the particular glass—whether it's blown or slumped or cast.

above These are what Morris calls "tippy-toe fish," created to be a presence at the bar in Granita, but not to block views.

LOCATION: **Malibu, California** INTERIOR DESIGNER: **Barbara Lazaroff** LIGHTING DESIGNER: **Pam Morris Designs: Exciting Lighting**
PHOTOGRAPHER: **Martin Fine**

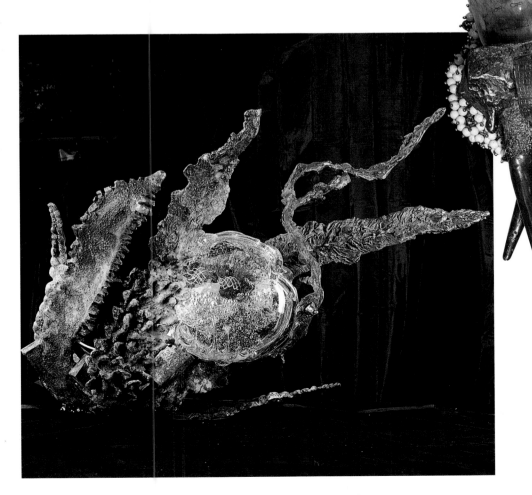

right Granita's "dancing pods" are tilted sideways as if swimming toward the surface of the sea.
below Granita's theme is aquatic and the custom luminaires seem like magical creatures captured in a moment of movement.

left Zenzero embodies a contemporary blending of European and Asian influences. **below** The backlit wood ceiling seems visually to float. **opposite** The bar area is distinguished by egg-shaped decorative luminaires.

Located in Santa Monica, California, Zenzero blends European and Asian influences. The contemporary space, designed by architect Charles Cordero, is highlighted by unusual finishes that include laminated rice paper, crackled glass, granite, and clear-stained wood.

The lighting design also blends varied elements. Giant egg-shaped glass and metal sconces are positioned in each corner of the bar area. These eye-catching decorative elements are in contrast to the layers of architectural lighting effects that play with the horizontal planes of the dining room beyond.

Lighting designer Celeste Gainey uses cold cathode, PAR 38s, purple neon, and MR 16s directly and indirectly to accentuate the clean-lined architecture of the space. The slightly curved, smooth wood ceiling suspended over the bar area is backlit with cold cathode that allow it visually to float. The bar area and dining room are dramatically separated with

AR 7 lamps built into a crackled-glass partition.

A single row of wallwashers is used to uniformly illuminate a wall of artwork. The lighting design emphasizes the cleanly articulated planes of the architectural elements. The textural decorative luminaires included

in the bar are in contrast to the absence of visible fixtures in the dining area beyond. Light from linear coves and circular downlights surrounds and envelops without overwhelming.

LOCATION: Santa Monica, California OWNER: Kurumaya U.S.A., Inc. ARCHITECT: Charles Cordero, AIA LIGHTING DESIGNER: Celeste Gainey, Gotham Light & Power Co. ELECTRICAL CONTRACTOR: Allspark, Electric LIGHT ARTIST: Pam Morris Designs: Exciting Lighting (bar sconce sculptures) PHOTOGRAPHER: Tom Bonner LIGHTING MANUFACTURERS: Neotek—cold cathode, Hydrel, Lightolier, LSI, Norbert Belfer, Artemide, Modular

left Artwork is uniformly illuminated with a single row of wallwashers.

right Lighting designer Celeste Gainey wanted to use light in layers to reveal architectural planes.

above An illuminated panel of crackled glass separates the bar area from the dining room.

ENTERTAINMENT
ENVIRONMENTS

TATOU BEVERLY HILLS

Tatou Beverly Hills—like its Tatou cousins in New York and Aspen—recreates the tradition of the hot nightspot that's the place to see and be seen. It was, in fact, inspired by the Coconut Grove nightclub, popular in the 1930s.

Jay Haverson and David Rockwell, formerly of Haverson/Rockwell and currently with Haverson Architecture and the Rockwell Group respectively, have used a variety of lighting fixtures to fill a neutral colored space with color and sparkle.

Their goal was to realize an environment in which guests could feel as if they were transported to another place in another time. At the same time, the space had to attract clientele for lunch, dinner and late supper servings.

The basic colors of the wall coverings and cloth hangings are neutral-beige, white and gold. To maintain as much of the ceiling height as possible, the space behind the fabric ceiling tents is kept shallow. MR 16 light strips which are capable of rendering the ceiling in three different colors, have been installed to backlight the soft gathers of tented fabric and evenly illuminate the entire area. Track lighting units fitted with color filters and positioned above the antique crystal chandeliers also light the fabric.

Around the perimeter of the room are ten custom-cast, patinated copper palm trees structurally integrated into the floor. The glowing clusters of coconuts, created by Karen Atta, are made of fiberglass with colored A-lamps concealed in them. Fiber-optic lighting, tucked into ridges in the trunks, allows the line of trees to wash

above The metal "Tatou" letters are backlit with yellow and red neon.
opposite Custom-designed palm trees glow with fiber-optic lit trunks.

LOCATION: **Beverly Hills, California** LIGHTING AND INTERIOR DESIGNER: **Rockwell Architecture, Planning & Design, P.C.**
ARCHITECTS: **David Rockwell, Jay Haverson, Sherrod Marshall, Wade Johnson, Mark Piccotto, James Ahn, Alice Yiu**
CONTRACTOR: **Turner Smith Co.** LIGHTING/AUDIO: **Markus Audio & Lighting Systems** PHOTOGRAPHER: © **Paul Warchol**
LIGHTING MANUFACTURERS: **Litelab, Sirmos, Altman, Diversitronics and Lightolier**

the space in changing colors, from red to amber to deep blue. The tropical theme is carried to the individual tables, as each has its own miniature custom-designed palm tree lamp.

The sophisticated control system allows for color changes and dimming of both the ceiling lights and palm trees.

In the corridors and bar area, existing recessed downlights have been relamped. Custom-designed, shell-shaped sconces have been added to the corridor and help to create a visual decorative rhythm along the wall.

The exterior facade sets the tone for the carnival of colors within. The metal letters that spell out "Tatou" above the entrance are backlit with a yellow neon strip which is beset by an added strip of red neon.

left Opaque, shell-shaped sconces adorn the wall opposite the bar.
below Recessed downlights illuminate the more subdued bar area.
opposite Clusters of coconuts are lit from within by A-lamps.

LE CLUB

Le Club is an unusual lounge/bar in that it has low seating and small tables with no bar to lean against or bar stools to sit on. The interior designer, Shigeru Uchida of Studio 80, opted to leave the room intact and use his own original furniture and lamps in the space.

The chair design, called "NY Chair II" by Uchida, is made of upholstery and steel with a baked melamine finish. It is a permanent collection piece at the San Francisco Museum of Modern Art. The tables are darkly colored, as are the walls, ceiling and floor.

The particular ambience of this minimally furnished space is created with patterns of light and shadow suffused through the perforated plates of the lighting fixtures. The fixture is made of steel with a baked melamine finish. Attached to the main body is a perforated aluminum plate, also with a baked melamine finish. It is lamped with a 100-watt halogen light source. In Le Club, the luminaires have been mounted to the floor and are positioned in groups of three at varied heights and angles.

Free-standing lamps, similar to those used in this bar, have become a part of the permanent collection at the San Francisco Museum of Modern Art as well. Originally called the "L-300," the luminaire was subsequently renamed "Tenderly" by Uchida.

As can be seen in the photos, Le Club truly explores the effect of the medium of light in space and on objects. The light fixtures not only serve as fixed architectural elements, but provide the most visual interest in the space. Grid-like patterns are projected in distorted shapes and intensities, depending on luminaire placement and height, on the neutral walls and ceiling.

The space is a study in contrasts between light and dark, low-lying furnishings and illumination cast high above it. The lighting at once reveals, enlivens and unifies the environment.

above Patterns of light are projected on the ceiling by lighting transmitted through perforated metal plates.

LOCATION: **Roppongi, Tokyo, Japan**   INTERIOR AND LIGHTING DESIGNER: **Shigeru Uchida, Studio 80**   PHOTOGRAPHER: **Hiroyuki Hirai, Hiroyuki Hirai Shashin Jimusho**

left A freestanding
fixture designed by
Shigeru Uchida has been
modified and fixed to
the floor of Le Club.
above This unusual
lounge is a study in con-
trasts: light and dark,
low furnishings and high-
mounted light sources.

THE DERBY

Perhaps the most striking aspect of The Derby is its ceiling. The previous restaurant that occupied the space had a 9-foot ceiling, and when the ceiling skins were peeled away during the renovation, the beautiful and intricate dome was revealed. The great, domed room measures 30 feet high and 70 feet across.

"Since the truss system in the ceiling dates from the 1930s, the structure was not sturdy enough to comply with today's more stringent codes for recessing lighting fixtures, so a means to light the space had to be devised other than recessed luminaires," says architect James Weiner.

Due to the client's budget constraints, the design team opted to "promote the volumetric phenomena," Weiner explains, and create The Derby's rich atmosphere using lighting and color. The main room, for example, is dressed in amber and gold at the top, and purple, violet, blue and burgundy at the floor level, with the lighting fixtures adding color as well as sparkle.

In the main room, a row of velvet-curtained booths line the central wall rising to the top of the dome. These booths are gently lit by Miss Sissi table lamps in jewel tones positioned on the low shelves behind the booth seats. On the walls above the tables, halogen-lamped Nelly sconces wash the lower portion of booth walls. Nelly pendants provide highlighting elsewhere in the club as well.

Weiner used groups of three bullet floodlights, typically used outdoors, but here lamped with a mixture of spots and floods atop the piers of the booths to uplight the breathtaking stained wood structure of the domed ceiling. The entrance to each booth is marked by a Collier halogen pendant which glows with colored glass rods and places a small pool of glare-free light on the carpet before each booth. Rising above the booths, and essentially dividing the building between The Derby nightclub and the adjacent Louise's Trattoria restaurant, the back wall soars to the full height of the dome. This wall pattern and shape is lit by a Giovi fixture, creating a sunburst effect which draws the eye to the ceiling.

An antique statue lamp of a woman holding a Venetian glass globe is the centerpiece of the horseshoe bar. Placed over the bar and throughout the room, recessed incandescents and adjustable recessed halo-

above At the banquet room bar, colored glass trims sparkle with illumination from the recessed downlights behind them.
below Table lamps in jewel tones add a soft glow to booth interiors.

LOCATION: **Los Feliz, California** ARCHITECT AND LIGHTING DESIGNER: **James Weiner Architect** LIGHTING CONSULTANT: **Chip Israel, Lighting Design Alliance** ELECTRICAL ENGINEER: **Amelect** CONTRACTOR: **Dan Barling** PHOTOGRAPHER: **Tom Bonner** LIGHTING MANUFACTURERS: **Leucos, Koch & Lowy, Flos and Artemide, Alkco, Halo, Capri, Stonco**

above Clusters of fixtures atop booth partitions cast patterns onto the intricate ceiling.

gens illuminate the main room and the peripheral seating areas, as well as the dance floor. An arc of halogen fixtures with glass shades in two different colors hovers, planet-like, along the bar.

The lighting scheme for the banquet room is elegant in its simplicity. At the entry and at the formal edge of the bar, Weiner used a row of recessed incandescent fixtures with colored glass trims to provide bright spots of color that glow on the ceiling and light the area below with a diffuse spot. The same fixture is used in the main room of the nightclub. A recessed halogen fixture with a mobile, crystal-glass shade illuminated by the light source glitters over the bar. Antique wall sconces with incandescent candelabra lights mark the perimter of the room, and recessed incandescent fixtures are scattered over the entire area.

above This lower ceiling in the banquet room contains recessed downlights and a row of downlights fitted with decorative trims.
left Pools of light are cast in front of each booth by halogen units suspended on stems.
opposite Globe-like pendants hover like planets in the sky.

SHERATON GRAND BALLROOM

The illumination for the ballroom addition to the Sheraton Hotel near the Dallas/Fort Worth airport had to be versatile to suit a variety of occasions. The space would be used for meetings, product shows, receptions and dinners.

In spite of the required flexibility, the lighting design team at Yarnell Associates had to retain the romance and traditional elegance of a classical ballroom. Their solution was to custom design chandeliers and sconces that provide functional lighting, while serving as decorative "jewelry" for the room.

Original luminaires have been created to avoid a standard catalog look. In response to the four different ceiling coffer sizes, a family of chandeliers has been developed to synchronize with the proportional requirements of each coffer. The range of styles and sizes within the fixture family also helps to avoid the typical visual boredom that sets in when one design is used over and over throughout a space. The smallest chandelier is approximately

3 feet, 6 inches in diameter.

Luminaire height also has been varied to increase visual interest. Chandeliers in the center of the room are shorter and broader, while those at the perimeter are longer and narrower. The classical styling of the chandelier emphasizes the crystal and minimizes the effect of the metal framework.

The crystal, selected from the more commercial and economical product available to meet budget requirements, includes octagonal beaded chains with colonial prisms used on the borders. Baskets of beaded crystal

are attached to the main body, and candles in clusters of three fill the baskets. The chrome interior metal structure complements the sparkle and whiteness of the fixture.

The chandeliers are complemented with two different wall sconce designs as well. Lamps, mostly long-life 25-watt A-19s, are positioned within the body to maximize the sparkle of the crystal. The jewelry effect of the luminaires is increased by the light blue neon coves installed around the perimeter of each coffer.

LOCATION: Dallas/Fort Worth, Texas   ARCHITECT: HKS, Inc.   LIGHTING DESIGNER: Bruce Yarnell and Derek Porter, Yarnell Associates   PHOTOGRAPHER: Gnuse/Coker Associates, Inc., Bruce Yarnell and Derek Porter

above   Depth and diameter of the luminaires vary. Those in the center are shorter and broader; perimeter fixtures are longer and narrower.

opposite top   The visual obtrusiveness of the metal chandelier framework has been minimized to allow the sparkling crystal to hold center stage.

opposite bottom   A family of fixtures, including chandeliers and wall sconces, has been custom designed for the ballroom.

DISNEY'S WILDERNESS LODGE

Walt Disney World in Orlando, Florida, is characterized by highly detailed and well-executed themed environments. Disney's Wilderness Lodge was to be a hotel in which guests could enjoy surroundings that incorporated researched historical themes and the artistry of Native American craftsmen.

The "storyline" for the hotel involves the look of the lodges of the great American Northwest. The time period reflected in the interior designs is 1900-1930s and includes design elements from the American Arts and Crafts Movement through the Teddy Roosevelt "Rough Riders" era.

Custom-designed chandeliers distinguish the atrium of the lodge. The 15-foot-tall luminaires are based on 18-inch-tall table lamps designed in the early part of this century by artist Thomas Moran. Genuine stretched leather has been fashioned to resemble a tepee. Native Americans hand-painted each chandelier with figures and symbols depicting their family histories. The iron framework includes animal and Native American figures frozen in motion.

Each chandelier includes two types of light sources. Standard A-lamps are housed in the tepees and provide a warm glow. Downlight is cast by MR 16s concealed behind an acrylic ring positioned just inside the iron perimeter near the fixture bottom. The acrylic has been faux-finished to resemble the painted leather.

To avoid a dark cavernous feeling in the high-volumed atrium, uplights have been mounted on the wood beams near the ceiling. They are placed inconspicuously to create the illusion that it is actually the chandeliers which are illuminating the entire space.

Additional fixtures mounted on the trusses are focused on artwork and architectural details that require accenting, such as the authentic hand-carved totem pole.

The sconces that run along

above The atrium is illuminated not only by the decorative chandeliers, but by uplights concealed on wood beams near the ceiling.

LOCATION: **Orlando, Florida** OWNER: **Walt Disney Company** ARCHITECT: **Peter Dominick, Urban Design Group** LIGHTING DESIGNER: **Chip Israel, Lighting Design Alliance** PHOTOGRAPHER: **Disney Development Company** LIGHTING MANUFACTURERS: **T.A. Greene, Cornelius Architectural Products, Alger**

left Native American and Northwest design elements enrich the luminaires' ironwork.
below Great attention to authenticity and detail was paid to painting leather and crafting chandeliers by hand.

the corridor walls on each floor of the lodge are ADA-compliant, flat acrylic discs with wire edging. The diffusers are painted with elements, such as buffalo, that extend the Northwest theme. There are two versions of these sconces: one is com-posed of one acrylic disc; the other version has two discs. Each sconce is lamped with compact fluorescents. The longer lamp life minimizes relamping for easier maintenance.

KOBE HARBORLAND NEW OTANI

The Kobe Harborland New Otani Hotel is located near Kobe Station in Japan. The Grand Banquet Hall includes three ringed chandeliers that embody the theme, "Jewels of Light." The chandeliers are made with 5.3m diameter reflecting panels that have a golden mirror finish, and varied-sized, wavy glass tubes and gold-laced piping arranged in 16 groupings in each circular chandelier.

Light sources used to illuminate the chandeliers include krypton and warm-white, high-intensity discharge lamps. One on/off and three intensity adjustment circuits per group permit flexible light levels to meet a range of functional and aesthetic needs. The indirect lighting feature creates the illusion that the chandelier is floating in air.

Twelve wall sconces that complement the style of the chandeliers are mounted on mirror panels that accent the walls of the room.

LOCATION: Kobe, Japan   ARCHITECT: Nikken Sekkei, Ltd.   LIGHTING SCULPTURE DESIGNER: Motoko Ishii, Motoko Ishii Lighting Design Inc.   PHOTOGRAPHER: Motoko Ishii Lighting Design Inc., Yutaka Kohno

above   The three chandeliers reflect the theme "Jewels of Light," and are complemented by matching wall sconces.

opposite   Each chandelier contains 16 groups of wavy glass tubes and gold-laced piping. Light levels can be varied to suit any occasion.

AMERICAN QUEEN

The American Queen Steamboat is a floating hotel that plies the Mississippi from New Orleans to Minneapolis and up the Ohio River to Pittsburgh. It was designed to capture the feeling of cruising down the river in the late 1800s in all its details, while incorporating the modern day conveniences and technology required for the operation of a hotel.

The 200 guest cabins include larger rooms which are furnished with antiques that not only date from the late 1800s, but are indigenous to the Mississippi River region.

Fortunately, the design team, which included Ronald Kurtz and Randy Burkett of Randy Burkett Lighting Design, Inc., was brought on to the project in the concept stage. Part of their challenge was to accurately specify the power requirements at the beginning of the project—the generators had to be designed to suit those parameters exactly.

Present-day safety codes also presented the designers with some limitations. For example, the use of wood was prohibited by fire codes. And most of the

fixtures not only had to meet UL requirements, but U.S. Coast Guard approval as well. Special connections were developed for the large chandeliers, for example, to keep them secure and in place in the roughest of water and weather conditions.

The public spaces on the steamboat that incorporate custom fixtures include the Grand Salon, the dining room, the lobby, and connecting spaces.

Many of the newly created decorative luminaires were inspired by photographs of chandeliers on boats from the period betweeen the late 1800s and early twentieth century. Gross Chandelier Co. proved a valuable collaborator on this project.

Most of the luminaires are incandescent light sources; many are candelabra-based A-lamps. The majority of the hotel's guests are age 50 and older, so high light levels were

top and above In the Grand Salon, theatrical lighting fixtures are tucked into a recessed panel around the ceiling perimeter. Carbon filament lamps are used around the perimeter and halogen lamps at crosspoints in the ceiling.

LOCATION: **Mississippi River**   LIGHTING DESIGNER: **Ronald Kurtz and Randy Burkett, Randy Burkett Lighting Design Inc.**   INTERIOR DESIGNER: **Al Luthmers, American Classic Voyages**   LIGHTING MANUFACTURERS: **Gross Chandelier Co., Light Solutions, Schonbek, Unilight, World Imports**   PHOTOGRAPHY: **Delta Queen Steamboat Co.**

required to accommodate the eyes of senior citizens comfortably. Efficient, flourescent fixtures are used in behind-the-scenes crew areas, however.

The chandeliers in the dining room are glass, as are the smaller fixtures in the Grand Salon. The larger decorative luminaires in the Grand Salon are made with acrylic in a faux alabaster design. Other decorative fixtures on board use linen shades and crystal ornamentation.

In the Grand Salon, several lighting systems are combined and benefit from connection to a dimming system. Fixtures using carbon filament lamps ring the proscenium and ceiling perimeter. Theatrical fixtures are tucked into coves around the ceiling perimeter and mounted above the giant chandeliers as well. At the center of each star in the crisscross ceiling molding is a halogen lamp for general illumination.

BIG CEDAR LODGE

The owner of Big Cedar Lodge, Johnny Morris, grew up in Springfield, Missouri, and in his youth enjoyed making fishing lures. According to lighting designer Craig Roeder, Morris' love of fishing led to his establishment of Bass Pro Shops—high-quality stores that offer the best in fishing and hunting gear.

About 10 years ago, Roeder says he became involved in the lighting of Big Cedar Lodge, located at Table Rock Lake, approximately 30 miles from Branson, Missouri. The success of the lodge has dictated continuous expansions since then. Its success is due not only to excellent service and an ideal location, but to the unusual architecture and design of this year-round sportsman's resort.

The wood and stone work project a rustic quality, yet at the same time the lodge reveals an ever-evident craftsmanship in its architectural elements and design so superb that it simply astounds. The resort was designed by the architecture department of the Bass Pro Shops' organization. The one-of-a-kind decorative lighting fixtures, which include wall sconces, pendants, and exterior luminaires, were created and built by the architecture department professionals and local craftsmen—a total of about 25 artists.

The luminaires, all projecting motifs drawn from nature, employ varied materials, from metal fashioned to look like leaves and glass colored to embody the color of sunset, to antlers, tortoise shells, and oddly shaped tree branches.

Not so obvious as the beautiful decorative fixtures are the architectural lighting elements Craig Roeder designed to illuminate space and accent architecture without revealing the sources of illumination. In fact, Roeder notes that the largest lighting fixture used is only 3 inches long and 1½ inches in diameter, and is hooded, louvered and painted so as to blend in and remain inconspicuous. Mainly quartz units have been mounted under and placed even at the bottom of fishing buckets to create soft ambient illumination in a room. The project is energy efficient, with light sources on dimmer.

above A combination of decorative and architectural lighting fixtures highlights the building exterior.

opposite Wood, stone and metal are warmed by the candle-like glow of luminaires.

LOCATION: Branson, Missouri ARCHITECT: Bass Pro Architecture INTERIOR DESIGNER: Edward Keith Interiors LIGHTING DESIGNER: Craig A. Roeder Associates DECORATIVE FIXTURES: Tom Jowett and Donald Briggs ELECTRICAL ENGINEER: Lottero and Mason Associates Inc. PHOTOGRAPHER: Bass Pro Shops LIGHTING MANUFACTURERS: Hydrell, Edison Price, Lite Lab Lite Touch, Norbert Belfer, Sterner, Hubbell

above The fixtures complement the rustic, woodsy quality of the room and its furnishings.
left Part of the richness of this Community Center room is the fact that not just one, but varied lighting fixture types are used: table lamps, pendants, sconces, and beam-mounted adjustable units.

above Lighting fixtures designed to suggest tree branches evoke the relaxing, golden glow of candlelight.

SEIJI OZAWA HALL AT TANGLEWOOD

Seiji Ozawa Hall at Tanglewood in Lenox, Massachusetts is a 1,200-seat enclosed hall used for music peformances, student recitals, rehearsals and commercial recording. Opening the folding doors at one end of the building allows patrons seated outdoors on the lawn to enjoy performances as well. Adjacent to the hall is a Performer Support Space.

The intention was to create a space that would have the intimacy of a smaller, existing hall designed by Eero Saarinen in 1941. Acoustic requirements led to the creation of the 50-foot-high hall, with thick side walls and a heavy, articulated ceiling.

The exterior reflects the simplicity, informality and restraint of the New England landscape in details such as the brick and timber side arcades, the wood grilles, and the curved roof of lead-coated copper.

The acoustics imposed three major requirements that affected lighting consultant Douglas Baker's design. First, neither the walls nor the ceiling could be penetrated. Next, the ceiling had to be heavily articulated. Finally, the lighting had to be

incandescent, except for some fluorescent strips backstage and in attic areas that are kept off during performances and recording sessions. This final requirement allows for dimming, while eliminating electronic interference or acoustical distractions when recording equipment is in use.

Ambient lighting is provided by PAR lamps mounted behind heavy, tempered glass plates in the ceiling, and shielded by a black louver. Accent and general lighting also comes from square and round custom pendant fixtures. These fixtures are clusters of incandescent lamps with

white acrylic diffusers. Some are accessed for relamping and maintenance from the attic; others are lowered on cables to floor level.

Areas beneath the high windows are lit by coves concealing A-lamp strips, and uplights and downlights on the upstage shutters. Small, narrow-beam PAR lamps on short stems illuminate the columns supporting the balcony girders. Bare tubular lamps in twin-socket fixtures mounted in the under-edge of the balconies afford illumination to the audience seated beneath the balconies.

above Glass doors and windows allow the audience to enjoy the summer landscape during performances.
opposite The simplicity of the wood grilles is echoed in the clean-lined pendant luminaire.

LOCATION: Lenox, Massachusetts OWNER: Boston Symphony Orchestra ARCHITECT: William Rawn Associates, Achitects
LIGHTING DESIGNER: Douglas Baker; IALD, Douglas Baker Lighting Consultant ELECTRICAL ENGINEER: Lottero and Mason Associates Inc. PHOTOGRAPHER: Steve Rosenthal LIGHTING MANUFACTURERS: Lighting Services Inc., Cw. Cole Co., Lithonia, Edison Price, Moldcast, Norbert Belfer, Strand and Swivelier

above Restraint and informality are embodied in the architecture and the straightforward lighting scheme.

above PAR lamps behind tempered-glass plates illuminate the stage area.

left An incandescent lighting system allows for dimming. Neither the walls nor the ceiling could be penetrated to accommodate the lighting for acoustical reasons.

PUBLIC SPACES

The University of Michigan, built in the early 1900s, has an architectural style reminiscent of Oxford—limestone exteriors punctuated with ornate gargoyles and other Gothic details.

The beautiful wood paneling in the classrooms and moot courtoom of the Law School are originals, but had become worn over the years and were in need of refurbishing. There had been an attempt in the 1970s to modernize the lighting system for the rooms, and consequently, four-by-four, gold-tone, parabolic luminaires were surface-mounted to the ceiling.

Quinn Evans/Architects, who have extensive experience in restoration projects, and Gary Steffy Lighting Design were commissioned to renovate the classrooms and courtroom so that they would reflect the rich historical character of the original design.

Custom-designed pendants have been created to complement the coffered ceilings. The acrylic diffuser bowls have been sandblasted to eliminate the sheen and produce a softer texture. The bronze detailing has been repeated from filigree and fleur-de-lis patterns found in

existing fixtures installed in other parts of the building.

Each pendant contains nine 39-watt compact fluorescents. Three are contained in the base of the bowl to provide downlight, and six are positioned near the top to cast light primarily upward. The light source was chosen because of the 19-foot-high ceilings. A considerable lumen package was required to illuminate the large volume, and

the compact fluorescents accomplish this in an energy-efficient manner.

Multiple switching options are available. Three controls offer pendant downlight only, and two additional levels of uplight.

Supplementary task lighting is provided by recessed PAR 30 and PAR 38 downlights. The PAR 38s are used mainly in the courtroom and the front of the classroom.

above The pendant bowls are made of acrylic, sandblasted to have a soft, matte finish.
opposite The large pendants contain nine compact fluorescents in order to provide enough light to illuminate the 19-foot-high space.

LOCATION: **Ann Arbor, Michigan** ARCHITECT AND INTERIOR DESIGNER: **Quinn Evans/Architects** LIGHTING DESIGNERS: **Gary Steffy and Gary Woodall, Gary Steffy Lighting Design** PHOTOGRAPHER: **Fred Golden** LIGHTING MANUFACTURERS: **Baldinger and Kurt Versen**

above Additional task lighting is provided by recessed downlights.

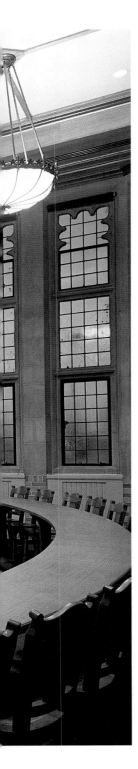

above Luminaires were custom designed to reflect the building's historical character.

left The decorative pendants were custom designed to include metalwork patterns found in existing fixtures elsewhere in the building.

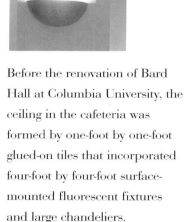

Before the renovation of Bard Hall at Columbia University, the ceiling in the cafeteria was formed by one-foot by one-foot glued-on tiles that incorporated four-foot by four-foot surface-mounted fluorescent fixtures and large chandeliers.

Since the style of the building that houses the cafeteria is Art Deco, the client requested the room be redesigned to reflect that style. When it came time to strip away the existing luminaires and ceiling, lighting designer Ann Kale discovered a pleasant surprise. Octagonal coffers from the original ceiling existed within 18 inches of where the new custom-made pendant luminaires were to be suspended. The design was modified to enable the pendants to be suspended from the center of the coffers. The coffers were painted to match the aluminum trim of the pendants for a unified look.

Each circular pendant has an opaque, acrylic diffuser and is fitted with eight PL 13 compact fluorescents. The pendants are circuited to allow for dual switching that enables either four or all eight lamps to be lit.

Two types of lighting are used in the lounge area. Semicircular aluminum sconces lamped with compact fluorescents are wall-mounted on the structural columns and provide uplight. The recessed downlights are also fitted with compact fluorescents. The only incandescent light sources in the room are used in the monopoint fixtures positioned to accent wall-hung artwork.

above Compact, fluorescent wall sconces and recessed downlights illuminate the lounge area.

LOCATION: **New York, New York**   OWNER: **Columbia University**   ARCHITECT: **Belmont Freeman Architects**   LIGHTING DESIGNER: **Ann Kale Associates, Inc.**   ELECTRICAL ENGINEER: **Mike Jacob, Atkinson Koven & Feinberg**   PHOTOGRAPHER: **©Arch Photo, Eduard Hueber**   LIGHTING MANUFACTURER: **Winona Lighting, Boyd, Edison Price, Lightolier, Halo**

above Custom-made pendant luminaires are suspended from the re-discovered octagonal ceiling coffers.

OHRSTROM LIBRARY

St. Paul's School is a traditional New England boarding school with a village-like campus. When the trustees decided to build a new library, a prominent site at the center of campus was selected. The library was to be a blending of the past and the present. It had to incorporate state-of-the-art, computerized information retrieval technology into traditional-style reading rooms that contained a variety of niches for individual or group study within easy reach of the bookstacks.

To complement the interior atmosphere of the building, the architects requested a decorative lighting system that might have appeared at the turn-of-the-century, yet adheres to today's energy and light level requirements, and necessitates minimal openings into the ceiling plane.

The lighting designers chose to make extensive use of fluorescent light sources to achieve required light levels at two watts per square foot and to ease maintenance via the lamps' long life.

To establish the visual aesthetics of early-20th-century fixtures and fulfill varied task needs, the lighting designers created a family of fixtures—including a small pendant, and table and floor lamps—each using a glass cylinder illuminat-ed with a compact fluorescent lamp as the base. To achieve the effect of the warm glow of traditional incandescent, mock-ups were produced that tested varied glasses and theatrical gels. Finally, a custom color and diffusion process was implemented that modifies the color and quality of the fluorescents to achieve the incandescent-like aura.

Location of these fixtures

above The chandeliers are lamped efficiently with compact fluorescents.

LOCATION: Concord, New Hampshire   ARCHITECT: Robert A.M. Stern Architects   LIGHTING DESIGNERS: Francesca Bettridge, IALD, and Carroll B. Cline, FIALD, Cline Bettridge Bernstein Lighting Design Inc.   ENGINEER: John L. Altiere Consulting Engineers   PHOTOGRAPHER: © Peter Aaron, ESTO   LIGHTING MANUFACTURERS: Bergen Art Metal, Linear Lighting, Harry Gitlin, and Edison Price

The turn-of-the-century styling complements the traditional architectural details.

within the library was carefully planned to reach appropriate reading light levels. All ceiling fixtures use a PL 26 quad compact fluorescent. Picture lights have been mounted over perimeter bookstacks to balance the light in the room and provide a glow on the rich wood-work. Three glass cylinder pendants illuminate the main reading room and use less than two watts per square foot. They are fitted with 16 compact fluorescents and eight low-voltage, angled spotlights.

In low-ceilinged areas, a central diffuser has been added. A PAR 38 downlight is used to project direct light over tables.

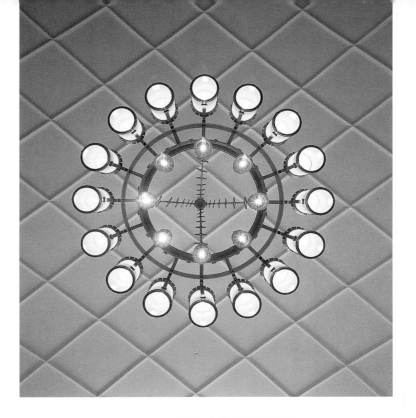

right The family of
fixtures revolves
around the basic compo-
nent of a glass cylinder.
below Picture lights
mounted over bookcases
balance the lighting in the
room and cast an enriching
glow on the woodwork.
opposite Custom fixtures
include pendants, and table
and floor lamps.

57TH STREET LOBBY

This small lobby serves as the entrance to a high-style building on Manhattan's 57th Street between Fifth and Madison Avenues—a fashionable shopping district. The entire lobby has been renovated, including the curved ceiling, which is made with sheets of stainless steel.

Edwin Rambusch, fixture designer and craftsman, was introduced to the building owner by lighting consultant, Claude Engel, and given the task of creating lighting fixtures that would take advantage of the unusual wall niches in the space.

Rambusch opted to fill the vertical slots with brass and slumped acrylic panels. Behind the panels in each niche are concealed two Biax compact fluorescent, 27-watt, 3,500 degree Kelvin lamps. The lobby is illuminated with direct light cast through the translucent elements, and indirectly from the metal-sheathed niches.

Visually, the niche fixtures establish an architectural rhythm from the front to the rear of the lobby. The luminaires function well both in the daytime—providing enough illumination to create a comfortable transition from bright daylight to the enclosed space, and at night—projecting an attractive image of glamour to those passing by the building.

The option was taken to design custom fixtures rather than specify standard luminaires in order to match the fixtures as closely as possible to the interior design scheme. Since the decorative luminaires are the only source of light in the space, custom design insured that a high enough level of illumination would be emitted from the decorative elements.

left Each fixture contains two, 27-watt Biax compact fluorescent lamps.

opposite The wall-niche fixtures are made with slumped acrylic and brass.

LOCATION: **New York, New York** OWNER: **Irene Duell, Morgan Holding** LIGHTING DESIGNER: **Edwin P. Rambusch, Rambusch Decorating Company** PHOTOGRAPHER: **Bill Rothschild**

OSBORNE HOUSE APARTMENTS

Over 100 years ago, architect James E. Ware captured the spirit of the Gilded Age at its height when he designed the Osborne Apartments on 57th Street in New York City. The elaborate Renaissance Revival lobby, restored by Rambusch Company, stands in contrast to Ware's exterior classical and Chicago-style stonework.

Though the mosaic and marble surfaces of the lobby were cleaned in the 1970s, subsequent deterioration of plasterwork and paint prompted a full-scale restoration of the space and reworking of its lighting.

A range of typical problems in architectural restoration were encountered. Project manager Martin Rambusch, and lighting renovation project manager, Edwin P. Rambusch had to preserve the interior's integrity by retaining the existing antique luminaires. The three chandeliers, however, had to be upgraded to meet today's energy code and safety requirements, and to meet the client's demand for higher illumination levels.

And though the existing sockets recessed in the canopies against the ceiling were too small and shallow to accommo-date new standard sockets, enlarging the holes would risk damaging the chandeliers' delicate wood, molded plaster, and repousse metalwork. Instead, the chandeliers have been cleaned and the original solid brass units have been rewired into the canopies.

The pendant socket recesses were large enough to contain new U.L. listed sockets. The dim incandescents in the hang-ing pendants and the canopies have been replaced with 60-watt clear incandescent bulbs.

The original pendants were designed to cast light down, leaving the ornate ceilingwork in shadow. This uplighting problem was solved by concealing four 27-watt compact fluorescents behind the wreaths crowning the main bodies of the chandeliers.

above The Gilded Age comes to life again with the restoration of the Osborne Apartments' lobby, designed originally by architect James Ware over 100 years ago. **opposite** Chandeliers were cleaned and rewired. The dim incandescents in the pendants and the canopies were replaced with 60-watt, clear incandescent bulbs.

LOCATION: **New York, New York** ARCHITECT: **James E. Ware** LIGHTING RENOVATORS AND DESIGNERS: **Edwin P. Rambusch and Martin Rambusch, Rambusch Decorating Company** PHOTOGRAPHER: **Bill Rothschild**

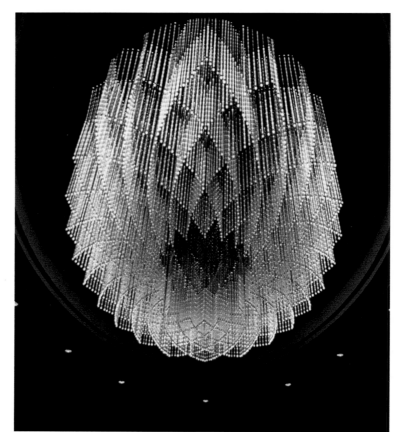

TAISEI HEAD OFFICE BUILDING

The renovation of Taisei Head Office Building in Tokyo included the installation of an optical fiber light sculpture to enhance the reception lobby of the directors' floor. The sculpture is 2.6m long and 1.5m wide, and contains approximately 1,800 optical fibers. The thin fibers create a visual perception of delicacy and refinement and are precisely arranged in scallop-type patterns.

The fibers are illuminated via four light source boxes, each containing four 100-watt, 12-volt halogen lamps. By controlling a rotating drum, light patterns can be varied for each season of the year.

above Light intensities and patterns are varied for each season.

LOCATION: **Tokyo, Japan** ARCHITECT: **A&T Associates** LIGHTING DESIGNER: **Motoko Ishii Lighting Design Inc.**
PHOTOGRAPHER: **Akihisa Masuda, Motoko Ishii Lighting Design Inc.**

Unobtrusive downlights surrounding the sculpture provide ambient and functional lobby illumination.

OTEMACHI AND KIOI-CHO

Intriguing corporate images can be created when strong and durable concrete and stone are juxtaposed with the sparkle and shine of decorative fixtures. Here are two examples of how contemporary, complex fixtures bring life to office buildings abroad.

The Otemachi Financial Center is located in the heart of Tokyo's financial district. It has been renovated and updated to function as an "intelligent" building. The lower stories offer a public usage link to the surrounding area and the subway.

The light sculpture, entitled "Tapestry, Harmony of Light," was designed by Motoko Ishii to enhance the open space from basement to third floor.

The sculpture is made with a blending of gold, silver and bronze pipes. Computer-controlled, multi-colored light created by special glass and halogen lamps weave a sculpture that seems to "breathe" as it rhythmically sparkles. Complement-

ary wall sconces for the exterior, first-floor lobby and basement are made of stainless steel and glass.

The Kioi-cho Building, located in Tokyo, is an "intelligent" office building that includes both commercial facilities and residences. The light sculptures in the entrance hall are designed by Motoko Ishii to harmonize with the architecture. The ceiling sculpture is made

with a mirror-finish, stainless steel ceiling plate and clear glass pipe. It is illuminated with 116 40-watt krypton lamps and one 250-watt metal halide lamp.

left The Otemachi "Tapestry, Harmony of Light" sculpture is made with gold, silver and bronze pipes. Halogen lamps make it sparkle. *opposite* The Kioi-cho building ceiling sculpture, made with a mirror-finish stainless steel ceiling plate and glass pipe, is illuminated with krypton and metal halide lamps.

LOCATION: **Tokyo, Japan**   ARCHITECTS: **Kume Architects-Engineers (Otemachi Financial Center), Mitsubishi Estate Co., Ltd. (Kioi-cho Building)**   LIGHTING DESIGNER: **Motoko Ishii Lighting Design Inc.**   PHOTOGRAPHER: **Yoichi Yamazaki (Otemachi Financial Center), Motoko Ishii Lighting Design Inc. (Kioi-cho Building)**

SHOPS AND SHOWROOMS

UNIVERSITY MALL

The renovation of the 20-year-old University Mall in Tampa, Florida included the new design for the interior and exterior by Anthony Belluschi Architects, and the development of an environmental graphics program by the Cincinnati office of Fitzgerald Roche Cicio & Hambrecht (FRCH) Design Worldwide. The graphics program incorporates lighting into the decorative elements used to revitalize and restore excitement to the 1.2 million-square-foot regional mall.

The environmental graphics program used three elements of Florida lifestyle as inspiration for the motifs: the sun, the moon and the ocean. The center court's visual vibrancy is due in large part to the nautical theme expressed in impressionistic wave forms made of aluminum and sign foam suspended from the ceiling in a spiral pattern. Running through the waves are colored lines of neon. Ceiling-mounted fixtures sparkle like the sun hitting the top of the ever-fluctuating sea. Bright orange and yellow fish fabricated out of sign foam are suspended in space, figuratively

swimming in all directions beneath the sea. Containing this visual sea are a ring of columns, lit at the top with bands of neon. At floor level, the illusion is completed with wave-shaped fountains near the built-in seating and planters in the center of the court.

The two new side courts playfully express the sun and moon themes. In the west court, an illuminated, abstract sun chandelier is suspended from the

center of the ceiling cove; in the east court hangs the moon chandelier. The sun and moon fixtures are made of frosted plexiglass and are attached to the skylight above by polished and painted stainless steel brackets. The chandeliers are surrounded by tapered columns decorated toward the top with layered, cut aluminum tree forms. The forms are highlighted with colored neon.

above University Mall's renovation included a graphics program with a logo using the Florida sun as its motif.
opposite In the central court, neon and ceiling-mounted fixtures represent sea waves and the glint of the sun on the water's surface.

LOCATION: Tampa, Florida   ARCHITECTS: Anthony Belluschi and Mike Sullivan, Anthony Belluschi Architects   LIGHTING DESIGNER: Gerry Zekowski Lighting   INTERIOR DESIGNER: FRCH Design Worldwide   PHOTOGRAPHER: George Cott, Chroma Inc.

The west court is enlivened by a chandelier that represents the sun.

left Waves of neon are attached to blue and green aluminum sheets and suspended from the ceiling.

below The east court's focal point is a chandelier that represents the moon.

SCOTTSDALE MALL

The 20-year-old Scottsdale Mall in South Bend, Indiana, had seen better days and though it had a facelift in the early 1980s, it was greatly in need of renovation a decade later. The signs were unmistakable: an alarmingly low occupancy rate, a blurred identity and a lack of amenities—all conspiring to discourage visits from potential customers. The architects developed a plan to revitalize the mall by creating a new image and changing the design to simplify the circulation and add amenities, including a food court and multiplex cinema.

Midwestern themes have been chosen for the spaces to reflect the precious region in which it is located. The themes are drawn from the St. Joseph River which bisects South Bend, local architectural styles, and the landscape and wildlife of the American heartland. Decorative forms use natural materials and simple shapes.

The redesign has divided the 750,000-square-foot mall into a series of distinct courts interconnected by a unifying design theme. The designers raised the roof over the center court using structural steel and vertical glass curtainwalls. An abundance of natural light now enters the center of the mall for the first time since it was built. All of the courts are linked by gently winding corridors that widen and narrow, suggesting the St. Joseph River. The floors are covered with patterned, blue-green tiles, and the logo developed for the mall depicts birds flying over a river.

The decorative elements in the central court include colorful birds in flight suspended from the ceiling, light fixtures of orange and red glass shaped like birdhouses, metal banners with leaf and flower motifs, and an elevator tower framed in timber supports and glass panels to resemble a Midwestern silo. Hardwood benches, light poles adorned with leaf patterns and new plantings complete visual unification of the mall.

above top The colorful elevator tower represents the silos found in the farm fields of the American Midwest.
above right Light poles look like birdhouses, made from red and orange glass and illuminated from within.
above left Raising the roof and installing a bank of windows has allowed more light into the center court.

LOCATION: **South Bend, Indiana** LIGHTING DESIGNERS: **Craig Roeder and Robert Oakes, Craig A. Roeder Associates**
PHOTOGRAPHER: **Robt Ames Cook** ARCHITECT AND INTERIOR DESIGNER: **FRCH Design Worldwide**

AYRES

Flocks of birds and birdhouse light fixtures bring new life to the Scottsdale Mall in South Bend, Indiana.

Gordon's

GRAND CENTRAL OPTICAL

Commuters rushing through Grand Central Station in New York City will have no problem viewing the eyewear for sale at Grand Central Optical due to its thoughtfully planned lighting. The client required the eyewear be visible through the front window, and yet have a clean look maintained inside the store as well. Lighting designer Ann Kale designed a multilayered system for the renovated interior created by Freeman & Pizer Architects.

Particular challenges for the lighting designer involved avoiding glare from light fixtures and the many reflective materials used to create the shop's contemporary, clean interior. Also, eyewear itself is difficult to light because of the transparent glass lenses and thin, reflective metals and plastics used in the frames.

The decorative fixtures were used because the space required good ambient light and the owner wanted the space to feel bright. The circular fixture is lamped with energy-efficient, compact fluorescent, PL 13 lamps. The use of mirrors to try on eyeglasses required enough ambient illumination to insure that only soft light would be cast and no harsh shadows would be created under customers' eyes.

The standard fixture has an acrylic diffuser with a stainless steel band, semi-recessed into the ceiling. Each fixture is fitted with four PL 13 lamps that glow. The light is reflected off the glossy surfaces below to create a bright, pleasant environment.

The store has a 1950s modern look and the decorative fixtures complement the interior treatment. Also in line with the modern motif is an inexpensive industrial jelly jar fixture installed at the small, circular counter near the storage closets.

Recessed, architectural lighting elements are used to highlight the merchandise. The eyewear has been successfully accentuated on the back wall with track-mounted, tungsten-halogen spotlights. The existing track has been refitted to suit the limited budget of this moderate-cost project. The halogen PAR 16 fixtures add just the right amount of sparkle.

The air duct is visible in the room and neither funds nor space near the ceiling were available to conceal the duct. The best was made of the element by playing off its silvery sleekness to emphasize the

above The custom-designed display cases are lit with low-voltage, tungsten lights.
opposite The horizontal display cases are lit from the inside.

LOCATION: **New York, New York** ARCHITECT: **Freeman & Pizer Architects** LIGHTING DESIGNER: **Ann Kale Associates** PHOTOGRAPHER: **Christopher Wesnofske** LIGHTING MANUFACTURERS: **Louis Poulsen, Lightolier, CJ Lighting Co., and Light Solutions East**

above left The display case rolls away from the window.

above right The standard circular fixture has an acrylic diffuser with a stainless steel band which is semi-recessed into the ceiling.

clean look of the store's interior.

The horizontal display cases are lit from the inside. Under the top of the case towards the rear (employee side—remote from the customer) are mounted, fluorescent case lights. The eyewear rests on top of a frosted, ribbed shelf backlit to silhouette the frames and clearly illuminate their shapes. The top fluorescent light allows the customer to read the frame colors accurately.

The glass ribs, angled for proper viewing, are ½ inch wide in order to keep the frames in place. Another advantage of the custom-designed lower shelf is that when a customer is being fitted for tinted lenses, the lens can be viewed by holding it on the countertop and the color can be sharply perceived due to the diffuse light.

Light itself is used as decoration as evident in the streak of light emanating from below the horizontal display cases. The fluorescent tubes beneath the ribbed, frosted glass shelving are positioned toward the front of the case, so tiny holes were drilled in the case to allow angled streaks of light out.

The custom-display case in the front window is lit with tungsten, low-voltage lights. Many are needed since the less opaque a surface is, the less it will admit light. The downlights are not centered, but positioned slightly forward to graze light along the front of the product.

above Also in line with the modern motif is an inexpensive industrial jelly jar fixture installed at the small, circular counter near the storage closets.
left The store has a 1950s modern look which complements the interior treatment.

HAMMACHER SCHLEMMER

Retailer Hammacher Schlemmer has been in business for decades, beginning as a hardware store, and over time developing into a purveyor of unusual, innovative and high-technology merchandise. The client wanted both the well-respected tradition of the store and its current state-of-the-art merchandise to be reflected in the renovated interiors.

Consequently, traditional materials and elements of style were combined with contemporary lines and finishes. For example, the 4-foot-tall, main floor, pendant luminaires recall traditional bell-shaped diffusers, but are composed of juxtaposed solid, ribbed and sandblasted acrylic panels. Each pendant has two quadrants—two plexiglass panels are gently curved outside the stainless steel collar and brass banding, and two plexiglass panels run inside them. The pendants house A-lamps and are suspended from braided stainless cables.

This effect of balance achieved in spite of diversity is reflected in other elements of the store interior. The main floor consists of two sections— one side is made of sheetrock and has columns; the other side is paneled in wood.

In addition to the decorative pendants, the lighting includes the juxtaposition of concealed and revealed fixtures. The main floor and lower level contain recessed, incandescent downlights, rows of picture lights to illuminate merchandise in the wood-paneled areas, and concealed, fluorescent coves. The lower level also includes a custom fixture which contains a fluorescent uplight component, as well as the capability of adding standard track lighting units.

The renovation has produced a clearly articulated space that unites variety and balance to give the client the fresh, new look desired.

above Some displays are illuminated with exposed lighting fixtures, others with concealed units.
opposite The sides of the main floor are different, but balanced.

LOCATION: New York, New York   CONTRACTOR: Clark Construction   ARCHITECT AND INTERIOR DESIGNER: Byrns, Kendall & Schieferdecker, Architects   LIGHTING CONSULTANT: Jerry Kugler Associates Inc.   PHOTOGRAPHER: James R. Morse   LIGHTING MANUFACTURERS: Fayston Iron and Steel Works, and Lightron of Cornwall Inc.

SILK SURPLUS

The architect of Silk Surplus Scalamandré fabric store wanted it to feel comfortable, look attractive and incorporate a balance of ambient and direct light. Installing only recessed architectural fixtures in the two-floor space and using only direct light would have created too many light and dark contrasts—too many shadows.

The alabaster pendants on the first floor are fitted with incandescent lamps and cast a soft, ambient light. Daylight from skylights enlivens the showroom during the day; during evening hours, the skylights are backlit by exterior floodlights with high-color-rendering, high-pressure sodium lamps.

The fabrics are washed with more task-oriented fixtures: 3-inch sleek, suspended cylinders that house a series of 50-watt MR 16s.

On the second floor, chandeliers were chosen to complement the good color-rendering recessed merchandise display lighting. They provide indirect ambient illumination while surrounding the luxurious merchandise with an equally opulent atmosphere and easing the eye into the room's decoration, from the ceiling to the floor.

Display cases holding fabric trims are lit with 50-watt PAR 16 floodlights mounted 6 inches on center. Because they are concealed above the structural frame of the display area, the customer can't see the lamps or fixtures.

Recessed adjustable square fixtures project a touch of decoration with their brass trims. They are fitted with 50-watt MR 16 floodlights.

above On the second floor, chandeliers surround the luxurious merchandise with an opulent atmosphere.
opposite The alabaster pendants on the first floor are fitted with incandescent lamps and cast a soft, ambient light.

LOCATION: **New York, New York** ARCHITECTS: **Susan Sheldon and Tami Bitter** LIGHTING DESIGNER: **Ann Kale Associates Inc.**
PHOTOGRAPHER: **Stan Ries Photography** LIGHTING MANUFACTURERS: **Reggiani, Lightolier**

above Chandeliers furnish indirect, ambient illumination.

left Built-in display cases holding trims are lit with 50-watt PAR 16 floodlights mounted 6 inches on center.

opposite During evening hours, the skylights are backlit with high-pressure sodium floodlights.

PERFUMERY AT LIBERTY

The Perfumery Department in the Liberty store, is about 210 square meters. It occupies the eastern corner of the Tudor-style building and reflects the store's dual commitment to contemporary design and fulfilling customers' needs.

The management at Liberty urged the professionals at Branson Coates Architecture to go beyond conventional thinking in beauty product store planning. The perfume buyer, Lorna McKnight, envisioned a soft space that would relax customers, rather than one that would promote the hard sell normally associated with beauty products.

The space created by Branson Coates is at once sensual, comfortable and fluid. Customers are urged to become involved with the product in this small area through individual counters that extend from a long, back-display wall easily accessed for browsing. Under-illuminated glass-topped tables bring samples and testers from the window display into the main circulation area.

Finishes used suggest both glamour and comfort. Deeply flocked walls and rich, oak flooring contrast with the shining, silver-leafed ceiling. Large, handblown chemist bottles, designed by Nigel Coates and hand blown by Simon Moore Ltd., act as defining accents in the displays of the perfume and beauty product houses.

The custom light fixtures

above Columns become oversized torchieres as light emanating from the capitals makes silver leafing sparkle.

LOCATION: **London, England**   OWNER: **Liberty Retail Ltd.**   ARCHITECT, INTERIOR AND LIGHTING DESIGNERS: **Nigel Coates, Doug Branson, Gerrard O'Carroll, Allan Bell and Geoffrey Makstutis, Branson Coates Architecture**   CONTRACTOR: **Claremont Construction Ltd.**   PHOTOGRAPHER: **Steve White**   LIGHTING FIXTURES: **Nigel Coates**

left Toilette tables become decorative luminaires as they make glass bottles glow with uplight.

incorporated into the department include Nigel Coates' Spring Lighting. The fixtures are lacquered, natural finished and made with aluminum and steel. Each uses a 50- or 75-watt halogen lamp.

These delicate, light source holders are complemented by the square columns that provide uplight and sparkle on the metallic silver capitals and ceilings from floodlights recessed in the capitals.

BARNES & NOBLE BOOKSELLERS

The uniqueness of the space chosen to house the flagship Barnes & Noble bookstore in Skokie, Illinois, allowed the architects at Antunovich Associates to use the design themes and vernacular common to all of the chain's revamped stores and create a strikingly grand retail environment.

Of the 47,000 square feet of leasable space, only 10,000 square feet were located on the first floor; the remainder were in the basement level. The architects opted to eliminate 3,000 square feet on the first floor so that a high-ceilinged "grand hall" could be created in the basement level and is visible to the customer upon entry.

The first floor includes a cafe near the entrance, the cash/wrap area and a perimeter mezzanine of bookshelves and browsing space. Barnes & Noble's goal is to project an environment that combines the contemporary with a touch of quaintness. The lighting fixtures contribute significantly to this achievement. Large, cus-

tom-designed chandeliers made with acrylic panels held in a satin, brass-finish frame and accented with dark hardwood echo the prairie-style interior detailing.

In any retail situation, product has to be well-illuminated to sell, even on the bottom shelves. The high, approximately 27-foot ceiling intensified the need for adequate lamping which would cast enough light down and allow customers to not only read books, but perceive titles of books on the lowest shelves.

Each chandelier is lamped with ten, 39-watt biax fluorescent lamps that provide both task and ambient light. Several PAR lamps concealed in each chandelier are positioned to

uplight the ceiling in order to avoid a dark cavernous look and instead, create an overall bright and uplifting high-volume space.

Post-mounted acrylic lanterns fitted with A-lamps flank the staircases and complement the design of the chandeliers. The family of fixtures designed for this project also includes luminaires suspended over the cash/wrap area and fluorescent acrylic sconces mounted on the building's brick exterior.

As part of a mall, this Barnes & Noble had to compete with a variety of other shopping experiences vying for customers' attention. The quality image projected by the store's design makes it a retailing success.

above Acrylic and metal sconces mounted on the brick facade reflect the prairie-influenced style of the grand chandeliers in the interior of the bookstore.

LOCATION: **Skokie, Illinois**   ARCHITECT, INTERIOR AND LIGHTING DESIGNER: **Antunovich Associates**   PHOTOGRAPHER: **Jon Miller, Hedrich-Blessing**
LIGHTING MANUFACTURER: **NL Corporation**

far left Giant chandeliers are equipped with biax fluorescent lamps for ambient and task light, and PAR lamps for ceiling uplight.

left The fixture family developed for the store includes post-mounted lanterns that flank the staircase at regular intervals and adorn the mezzanine.

below Recessed downlights in the 27-foot ceiling supplement light from the chandeliers to provide adequate illumination for book reading.

JIGSAW

Jigsaw, King's Road and Jigsaw, Manchester clothing stores in England embody a design rationale that "combines contradiction" and in doing so reflect the continually evolving creative philosophy of Branson Coates Architecture. For example, warm wood flooring and handrailing is mixed with contemporary metal flooring and display unit details.

Concern for effective lighting design had been present from the beginning of the design phase. Custom fixtures designed for the stores include Nigel Coates' Spring Lighting units. These small pendants possess a delicate, yet high-tech look. The shot-blasted glass and steel fixtures are lamped with 50- and 75-watt halogens. They effectively illuminate merchandise below while adding pools of light to the ceiling and a hint of sparkle in the space.

Jigsaw, King's Road, is distinguished at its entrance by a video projection of the earth

spinning on a hemisphere screen mounted on the ground floor ceiling.

In the Jigsaw, Manchester, giant illuminated lightboxes have been created featuring specially commissioned photographs by Peter Fleissig with drawings by Stewart Helm superimposed on them. The artwork as well as the yellow bobbins on the Branson Coates-designed shelving and hanging system reference Manchester's

history as a world textile producer.

Task and ambient illumination is also provided by Spring Lighting units that, here in the Manchester store, are suspended on a circular ceiling-mounted tube.

LOCATIONS: **London and Manchester, England**   ARCHITECT, INTERIOR AND LIGHTING DESIGNERS: **Nigel Coates and Doug Branson, Branson Coates Architecture**   PHOTOGRAPHER: **Peter Fleissig**   LIGHTING FIXTURES: **Spring Lighting designed by Nigel Coates**

above Spring Lighting System by Nigel Coates is hung on circular ceiling tubing.

opposite A globe with a video projection of the earth is visible from the exterior of Jigsaw.

above Large, illuminated lightboxes feature photographs of a Manchester canal with a superimposed drawing by Stewart Helm.

CUSTOM AND
LUMINAIRES

DECORATIVE

TEXTURES AND MATERIALS

The quality of light depends not only on the light source, but on the materials used to diffuse and shape the light. The light source, in turn, affects the materials that are used as the diffusers. Products gathered here reflect the wide range of materials and light sources used in decorative fixtures today.

The rich, bold blues and reds, or the creamy opaque white of satiny, smooth Murano glass are given depth by the light source they shield. Crystal and leaded glass, long associated with decorative luminaires, grace both traditional and contemporary motifs.

Technology has allowed the use of treated papers, parchments, and fabrics that lend to luminaires a three-dimensional textural quality previously unavailable. The possibilities of metals have expanded today beyond popular polished and satin-finished aluminum and brass to include perforated screens and wire mesh diffusers that project strong or subtle patterns of light.

Marble and alabaster are joined by acrylic look-alikes and painted ceramics as decorative diffusers.

"Products

gathered here reflect

the wide range of materials

and light sources used in

decorative fixtures today."

Mr. Wizard/ Le Collezioni
Chris Poehlmann created The
Mr. Wizard table lamp. The
colorful luminaire is available through Antonio Conti
Le Collezioni. Le
Collezioni's goal is to
incorporate all the ele-
ments needed to bring
provocative, yet refined
collections of art to the
industry each season.

Colorshades/Face Lights
Face Lights' Colorshades are inter-
changeable mylar shades imprint-
ed with brightly colored designs
that produce a soft, diffuse,
ambient light and a jewel-like
illumination of the shade's colorful patterns. Inexpensive
and easily installed,
Colorshades bring to lighting the added dimension
of flexibility.

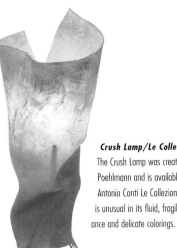

Crush Lamp/Le Collezioni
The Crush Lamp was created by Chris Poehlmann and is available through Antonio Conti Le Collezioni. The lamp is unusual in its fluid, fragile appearance and delicate colorings.

Pierce Lamp/Metalum   Metalum's fun and fashionable "Pierce Lamp" in three frame finishes: polished copper, chrome, and powder-coat black. The shades of these table lamps all have a metallic lining of either copper or silver. Combinations offered are black/copper, turquoise/silver, white/silver, red/silver, and dark-blue/copper. The overall dimensions are 5½ inches in diameter and 10 inches high. The power cord has a roller switch and the light source is a medium base, 40-watt torpedo.
*photograph by **William Pritchett***

Velo/Adesso Adesso's Velo/LT floor lamp includes an iron and brass sculpture frame and a bronze and mesh shade. It stands 71 inches high and uses a 100-watt bulb.

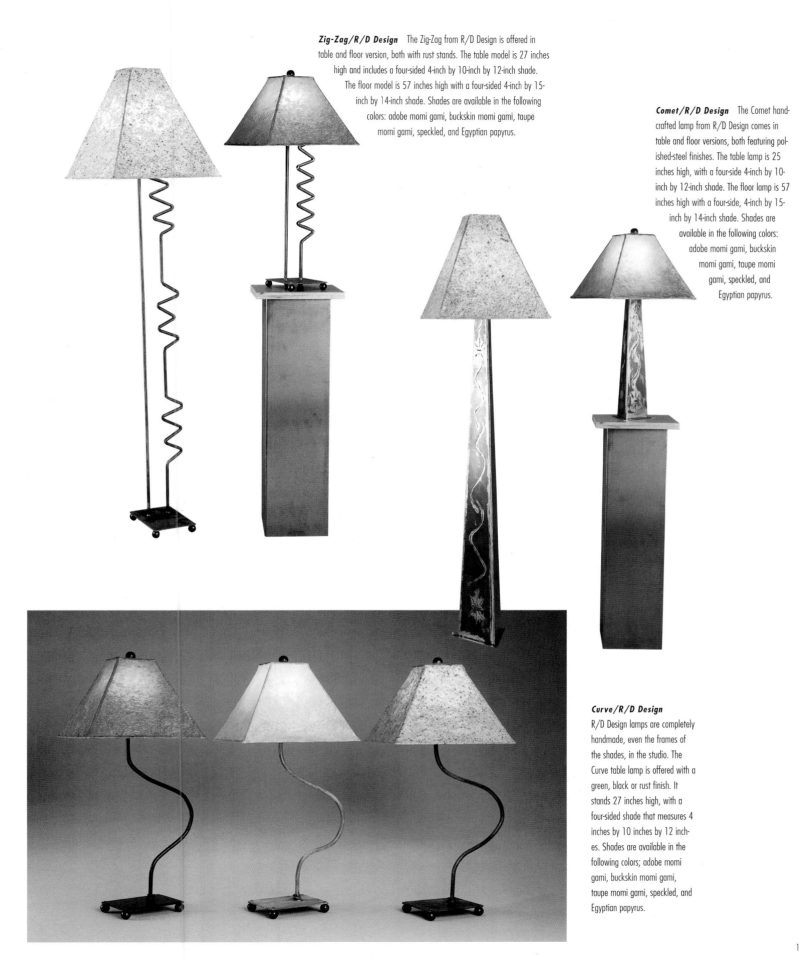

Zig-Zag/R/D Design The Zig-Zag from R/D Design is offered in table and floor version, both with rust stands. The table model is 27 inches high and includes a four-sided 4-inch by 10-inch by 12-inch shade. The floor model is 57 inches high with a four-sided 4-inch by 15-inch by 14-inch shade. Shades are available in the following colors: adobe momi gami, buckskin momi gami, taupe momi gami, speckled, and Egyptian papyrus.

Comet/R/D Design The Comet hand-crafted lamp from R/D Design comes in table and floor versions, both featuring polished-steel finishes. The table lamp is 25 inches high, with a four-side 4-inch by 10-inch by 12-inch shade. The floor lamp is 57 inches high with a four-side, 4-inch by 15-inch by 14-inch shade. Shades are available in the following colors: adobe momi gami, buckskin momi gami, taupe momi gami, speckled, and Egyptian papyrus.

Curve/R/D Design
R/D Design lamps are completely handmade, even the frames of the shades, in the studio. The Curve table lamp is offered with a green, black or rust finish. It stands 27 inches high, with a four-sided shade that measures 4 inches by 10 inches by 12 inches. Shades are available in the following colors; adobe momi gami, buckskin momi gami, taupe momi gami, speckled, and Egyptian papyrus.

Wave/Boyd The Wave wall bracket, designed by Erik Stanton Chan for Boyd Lighting Company, features translucent, European glass that is hand-slumped and softly satin-etched. The unit is accented with polished balls of chrome or brass and is available for incandesent or compact-fluorescent lamping.

photograph by Rick Mariani

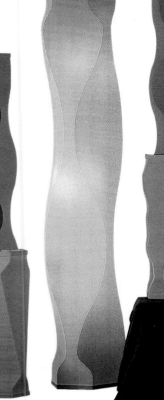

Lumalights/Interfold
Roland Simmons has created a series of luminaires, Lumalights, that are constructed of translucent, corrugated paper with washboard surface turned out that zip up for easy assembly. With the lights off, the fixtures become pure sculpture. When the candelabra lights within are turned on, a soft glow emanates. Lumalights from Interfold are offered in three heights: 32, 76 and 90 inches.

Scarlet/Azizi The Scarlet table lamp from Azizi combines metal with a textured paper shade and colored base. All Azizi products are designed and made in California.

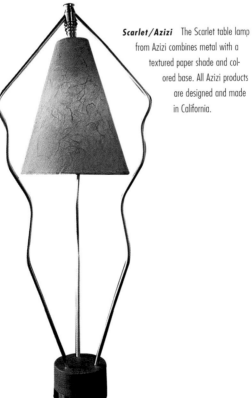

Patella/David D'Imperio The delicate, flower-like Patella Lamp created by David D'Imperio has a dyed wood shade, brass stems, ivory-lacquered wood and black base. The shade is available in yellow or green. The fixture stands 15 inches high and is 2½ inches wide. It uses a halogen lamp and comes equipped with a transformer and dimmer.

Ming/Lamps By Hilliard Janene Hilliard custom makes each tile in the Ming China table lamp by fusing a thread of black glass to a small rectangle of base glass. The tiles are then leaded together to form a pattern. The shade is 18 inches wide, and the overall height is 20 inches. Bases and support arms are solid cast bronze.

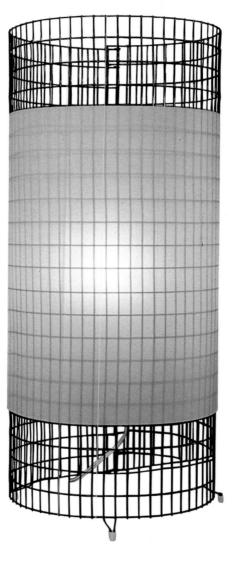

Wire Lamp/Z-Axis, Inc. Ronald Dhing's Wire lamp stands 22 inches tall and 9½ inches in diameter. It uses a 60-watt incandescent bulb with a mylar shade.

photograph by **Jim Foreman**

Leo Flame/Kane Shrader Leo Flame is intricately fabricated at Kane Shrader Custom Design, with a time-consuming, three-part casting, to bring out the depth and realism of a burning flame. The fixture is offered with a gold-leaf finish on plaster (shown) or in a clear resin.

Details/Justice Design Group

Details is a customizing program offered by Justice Design Group that provides 48 finishing options for the company's collection of ceramic wall sconces. Bisque, glazed and painted finishes include the classical look of quarried marble.

photograph by **Barry Elvove**

CONTEMPORARY

Included here are a range of modern European fixtures, as well as a number of American offerings. Although contemporary fixtures come from both large and small manufacturers, many of the cutting-edge concepts originate with individual architects and designers who either produce their own small line of fixtures, or who are commissioned by a larger manufacturer to create an original design.

Modern motifs tend to startle with unusual and often abstract shapes that are juxtaposed against the textures and qualities of the materials used to create them. Curving metal stems, glass globes of saturated color, perforated metal screens, copper and aluminum tubes, adjustable decorative suns on bare wires, plates of white glass, and smooth wooden floor lamp stems—all these elements combine to allow us to look at light in a new and different way.

These fixtures take an intangible, abstract element—light, the revealer—and attempt to capture it and hold it in glowing packages that extend our sensibility toward what light can be in relation to space and other objects in it, and what light is in itself.

"Modern motifs
tend to startle
with unusual
and often
abstract shapes..."

Streamers/Boyd   The Streamers pendant from Boyd Lighting Company
has a subtly etched, white, European glass diffuser that provides a
smooth, even surface for optimum light distribution and minimal glare.
Multiple height options are offered, with incandescent lamping standard.
Streamers' distinct character comes from leaded crystal drops and hand-
slumped glass ribbons in six colors.

*photograph by **Rick Mariani***

Options Series/SPI Lighting Inc. The Options Series pendant from SPI Lighting Inc. is 29 inches in diameter. Acrylic bottom shields are available in various shapes and colors to accessorize this standard fixture. A downlight accessory provides an accent pattern on the bottom shield. SPI indirect fixtures are specified for public spaces, merchandising areas, recreational interiors, education facilities and office environments.
*photograph by **Richard Beauchamp***

Uni-X/Luceplan USA The Uni-X family of luminaires from Luceplan USA includes a series of wall sconces. The basic Line model consists of an aluminum arm, available in anthracite and blue. The unit can be modified by adding diffusers to create the Glass, Plast or Globe models. Shown is the Glass version, fitted with a red diffuser that is also offered in white, yellow and blue.
*photograph by **Leo Torri***

Fenice/Adesso Adesso's Fenice table lamp includes a diffuser of antique blue Murano glass set in a frame of iron, brass and copper. The lamp is 17 inches high and uses a 150-watt halogen light source which is included.

Elissa Collection/Adesso   The Elissa Collection from Adesso includes table, floor, wall sconce and pendant models. Each version includes a Murano glass shade. The floor lamp is available in mahogany with chrome and copper, or a natural oak with matte-chrome finish. The table lamp, sconce and ceiling pendant come in chrome and copper, or matte-chrome finishes.

Dazzle/Artup Dazzle T-1025, created by the Artup design team, uses a 150-watt halogen lamp, and is constructed of cast aluminum, steel and glass. The light source housing and arm are available in white, black and gold finishes. The unit is 10 inches deep and 19 inches wide. The Dazzle Collection also includes pendant, wall sconce and floor models.

Eclipselipse/Ingo Maurer GmbH Ingo Maurer is renowned for avant-garde and trend-setting innovations in fixture design. Eclipselipse seeks to answer the questions: is art reflected in the form of the product? or does the product's form reflect art? The wall sconce's mirror and light source are 360 degrees adjustable. Adjusting their positions creates changing patterns.

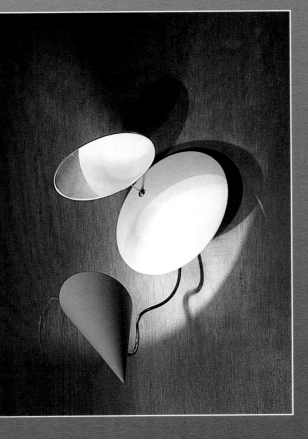

Aria/Optelma AG The Aria floor lamp from Optelma AG is 180 centimeters high and uses three 20-watt, low-voltage lamps. The metal stems are complemented by the opal glass diffusers.

MR 16 Series/David Bergman David Bergman's Fire & Water line of decorative lighting utilizes copper for an effect at once graceful and tough. The MR 16 Series uses exposed MR 16 reflector bulbs at the ends of copper tubes as an integral part of their design. The series includes ceiling fixtures and floor lamps. Some incorporate geometric angles and regular curves, while others swirl into exuberant compositions.

Calla Lily/David Bergman The Calla Lily series designed by David Bergman offers an organized image, joining gentle, stem-like curves of copper with mesh diffusers shaped into flowers. Available in several models, the Calla Lilies, as well as the MR 16s, can be custom designed to any specifications.

Sun Light/Expo Design The Sun Light low-voltage lighting system includes the vertical cable system shown with top and bottom mounted base, two 10-foot cables, and three 20-watt halogen sun fixtures. There are table light and wall sconce versions as well. The fixtures can be positioned along the cables (or bars of the table light and sconce) and tilted. Soft light streams from the front, back and sides of the sun.

photograph by **Bill Busch**

Aurora Borealis Table Lamp/Azizi The Aurora Borealis table lamp from Azizi turns the light source southward. Its zigzagging stem ends in a sturdy support system with three curved, metal legs.

Aurora Borealis Floor Lamp/Azizi Expect the unexpected in dynamic metal shapings from Azizi. The Aurora Borealis floor lamp, in brushed aluminum and brushed copper, twirls and curves its stem to support a cupped 300-watt halogen light source. The floor lamp is 73 inches high and comes with a floor dimmer.

REBORN CLASSICS

The beauty of decorative luminaires knows no time limits. Complementing the forward thinking of cutting-edge modern motifs are the craftsmen and manufacturers who draw the best from the past and apply it to today's sensibilities.

The Frank Lloyd Wright wall sconce and table lamps are accurate and faithful reproductions of what the renowned American architect created over half a century ago. Other companies enrich their decorative fixture lines by including traditional styles, such as French Art Nouveau, or by using techniques perfected in the past, such as repoussé.

Also popular, and yielding unending variations, is a kind of middle-of-the-road approach, in which manufacturers streamline and refine classic lines from the past to blend in with more modern decor.

"...craftsmen and
manufacturers
who draw the
best from the past and
apply it to today's sensibilities."

Portable Lamp/Visa Lighting Visa's quality design and construction has gone portable with its table lamp series. These lamps stand 28½ inches high and 22 inches wide with an 8-inch shade. Created with several configurations and classic shade options, these table lamps are available with incandescent or integrally ballasted, compact-fluorescent lamping. Options include brushed solid aluminum and painted finishes.

Sumac V/Yamagiwa Corporation Working with the Decorative Designs Collection which was established by the Frank Lloyd Wright Memorial Foundation at Taliesin West, the Yamagiwa Corporation reproduced 14 of the renowned archtiect's lighting fixtures. Wright designed interior furnishings as integrated components of the architectural whole, striving for a sense of unity in the domestic landscape. These pieces reflect the full range of Wright's creative genius: stylistic references vary from the fluid, organic renderings of nature to more austere and abstract geometric renderings of form. The Sumac V table lamp was designed in 1902 for the Dana Thomas House in Springfield, Illinois, and is a composition of rectangular panels of art glass set in a bronze frame with geometric patterning. It is 10 inches high by 5 inches wide.

Taliesin I/Yamagiwa Corporation
The Taliesin I table lamp was designed in 1925 by Frank Lloyd Wright for his own home in Spring Green, Wisconsin and was reproduced by the Yamagiwa Corporation. It has a square wooden base and roof-like shade, and measures 20 inches high and 14 inches wide.

Robi I/Yamagiwa Corporation
Reproduced by the Yamagiwa Corporation, the Robi I sconce was designed in 1906 by Frank Lloyd Wright for the Frederick Robi House in Chicago. Its white luminescent sphere, suspended in a bronze frame, conveys a sense of weightlessness. It is 11 inches high and 13 inches wide.

Tassel/Baldinger
Tassel is part of the Robert A. M. Stern Collection from Baldinger. The chandelier is shown in a 30-inch diameter model with polished nickel finish and frosted-white acrylic bowl. Other options are available.
photograph by **Peter Weidlein**

Trio/Lightolier The Lightolier ADA Wall and Corridor Fixtures are designed to meet the Americans with Disabilities Act's 4-inch projection mandate. The ADA line is offered in a broad range of styles, sizes and shapes (round, oval, square and rectangular) and are made in an equally broad combination of metal, glass, alabaster, acrylic and polycarbonate. The Trio model is shown.

Visor/Lightolier Every design in the ADA Wall and Corridor Fixture collection from Lightolier uses compact fluorescent lamps and many have the option of using standard incandescent lamps as well. All units, including the Visor model shown, have the lamp shielded on both top and bottom for comfortable viewing. Many of the fixtures employ Lightolier's exclusive rapid-start, noise-free, PowerSpec electronic ballasts.

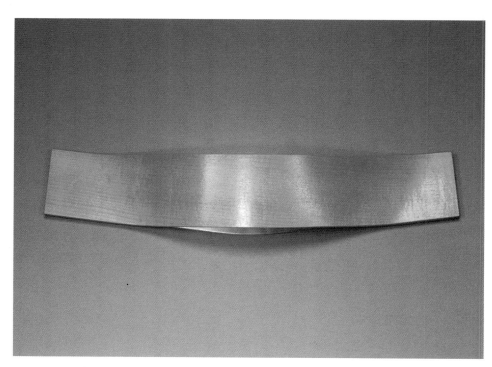

Surf/Baldinger Baldinger manufactures both standard and custom-designed fixtures. Surf, designed by Piotr Sierakowski, is part of the Baldinger ADA Collection, which contains luminaires that meet requirements of the Americans with Disabilities Act. Surf is $3\frac{1}{2}$ inches high, 20 inches wide, and projects $3\frac{1}{2}$ inches. The diffuser is offered in mahogany wood, maple wood or gold or silver leaf on maple wood. The unit is lamped with one PL 13, and must be mounted to a 2-inch by 3-inch horizontal gem box.
photograph by **Peter Weidlein**

Paladin/Boyd The Paladin pendant, designed by Jean Clyde Mason for Boyd Lighting Company, has an etched, white, European glass diffuser. This is paired with trimmings of gold or silver rope, or even the customer's own material to complement varied environments. Multiple height options and diffuser sizes increase design possibilities.

*photograph by **Swanson Images***

Lotus/Casella Repoussé is a method of hand hammering and buffing metal. The Norman Grag line of repoussé chandeliers, ceiling fixtures and sconces offered by Casella Lighting are custom-made works of art signed, sequentially numbered and dated by Norman Grag. The Lotus Chandelier is repoussé solid brass with a patina brass finish and is also available in solid nickel silver. It uses a 200-watt quartz lamp. The chandelier is 17 inches in diameter, and can stand 44 inches high or be made as a ceiling fixture.

photograph by **Grag Studio**

Venetian/New Metal Crafts New Metal Crafts specializes in antique reproduction and custom fixtures for homes and public buildings. The three-candelabra, custom, Venetian opaline fixture with gold accents and gold finished metal parts measures 19 inches high and 11¾ inches wide. It is also available with additional ceiling chain.

Emile Galle Series/Meyda Tiffany
The Emile Galle Series features table lamps reproducing the designs of prolific artist Emile Galle who was in the forefront of the French Art Nouveau design movement. The craftsmanship in the lamp includes the layering of different colors of mouth-blown glass into a mold to create the shape. Artisans hand carve the top layer of glass in various depths which results in several combinations of colors and embossed designs. The series features many color combinations including burgundy/pink, blue/pink and green/pink. The lamps range in height from 1 to 20 inches, with shade diameters from 7 to 16 inches.

Wall Mount/New Metal Crafts
This wall-mounted New Metal Crafts interior fixture is offered with verde and light antique brass or all-light antique brass. The luminaire from the top of the backplate is 13¼ inches high by 4½ inches wide. The one standard base lamp is 8 inches in diameter and extends 11 inches from the wall.

TECHNOLOGY
AND TECHNIQUE

The explosion in the development of kinds of light sources available in the past decade has had an impact on the design of decorative luminaires. Energy constraints and the popularity of the compact fluorescent lamp have led to the design of fixtures that can accommodate both incandescent and fluorescent sources.

The tiny halogen lamp has enabled fixtures to be created with equally tiny housings to envelop it. The emergence of bare-wire technology, and more sophisticated and flexible track systems, has led to a plethora of small, decorative elements that can often be adjusted and interchanged at will by the end user. Touches of color are possible with the addition of filters or dichroic reflectors.

No longer is decorative and functional light confined only to pendants, table and floor lamps, or wall sconces, but includes all of these and more—light suspended from trusses, tracks, cables and wires. This flexibility enables the designer to put a touch of decorative light almost anywhere.

"...flexibility enables the designer to put a touch of decorative light almost anywhere."

Micro Sconce/Casella The Micro Sconce houses a 9-watt PL mini-fluorescent light source in frosted Pyrex and solid brass. A ⅛-inch solid brass plate is a subtle backdrop for the cylinder. The fixture from Casella Lighting is offered in one or any combination of 12 finishes, including antique brass, polished brass, matte black, matte white, polished copper, oil-rubbed bronze, Casella bronze, polished chrome, antique zinc, silver plate, black nickel and verdi green. Designed to extend 3⅛ inches from the wall, the Micro Sconce complies with the Americans with Disabilities Act standards. It is switch-box mounted to accommodate the small backplate.

photograph by **Colucci Photography**

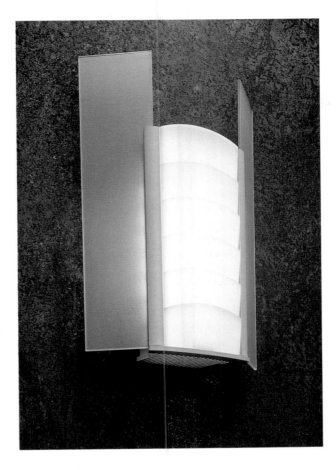

Aries/Flos   New to the Flight Collection and designed by Perry King and Santiago Miranda for Flos Incorporated, is the Aries line of ADA compliant, UL listed wall sconces. Three sizes are offered: a 14-inch-high model for use with either two PL 13-watt, twin tube fluorescent lamps or a 100-watt incandescent A lamp; a 17-inch-high version that uses a 27-watt Biaxial fluorescent lamp; and a 22-inch-high model that uses a 39-watt Biaxial fluorescent lamp. Each fixture has a central aluminum extrusion, with glass and plastic fittings. All have a white finish with plastic film inserts that cast a blue accent light if desired.

Masha/Artemide   The Masha wall fixture, designed by Jeannot Cerutti for Artemide, provides diffused incandescent or energy-saving fluorescent light. The diffuser is constructed in opaline white, handblown glass with chromed side fasteners. The body is concealed, white-lacquered metal mounted to a standard junction box. It measures 6$\frac{1}{4}$ inches wide, 13 inches high and projects 6$\frac{1}{4}$ inches.
photograph by **Artemide Inc.**

ADA Series/Manning Lighting   Manning Lighting offers a wide range of wall sconces that comply with the Americans with Disabilities Act requirements. All fixtures are UL listed, and most have a choice of operating with either an icandescent or compact-fluorescent lamp. All fluorescent fixtures have integral ballasts as a standard feature. The fixtures are available with painted finishes, polished brass, or chrome, and have options of white, faux alabaster, or green-edge clear acrylic.

Steel Feather/Tech Lighting   The Steel Feather from Tech Lighting creates a strong yet delicate impression with an interplay of color, texture and light. The unit can be secured to a vertical or horizontal cable. Included are two 20-watt halogen bipin bulbs. The diffuser is a fiberglass paper shade and can be ordered with or without a blue dichroic glass or other color glass filter. The back is chrome-plated, perforated steel. The chrome rods and sleeves are available in black or red.
photograph by **Ron Gurulé**

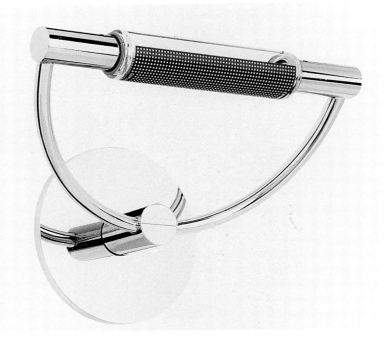

Litedisc/Lam Lighting Systems. Litedisc is a shallow-depth, ceiling-suspended pendant fixture which uses four compact-fluorescent tubes in an off-set-square pattern. A high-efficiency proprietary reflector system is positioned around the interior perimeter of the fixture. Specifiers may choose from four 40-, 50- or 55-watt compact fluorescent lamps. The pendant's design consists of two 20-gauge steel spinnings, an outer housing and trim ring, and an opalescent-acrylic luminous disc. Their combined depth is slightly over 6 inches. The disc's overall diameter is 39 inches. The outer housing is available in 11 standard, textured paint finishes that include white, warm white, red, blue, green, yellow, brown, medium architectural bronze, gray, black and satin aluminum. Optional finishes include brass plate or chrome.

photograph by **Georgia Brauer**

Gradi Miniparete/Cini & Nils Gradi Miniparete projects only 5⅛ inches from the wall, meeting demands of illuminating mirrors, hallways, staircases and other areas where minimum space and orientability are required features. The fixture is 8⅝ inches wide and offered in shiny chrome or burnished finishes.

Biz/Tech Lighting Biz MR 16 unit from Tech Lighting, Inc. has a slick, contemporary look. The Biz glass disk sits atop the exposed, secured MR 16 halogen bulb. A Biz Bang version is available with chromed counterweights that allow the unit to be moved up and down at will. Biz is offered for use with 20-, 35-, or 55-watt MR 16 halogen bi-pin lamps.

photograph by **Ron Gurulé**

T-Bar System/Translite, Inc. The T-Bar System is an open-conductor, low-voltage track lighting system. Its strong construction and geometry allow for long spans, with minimal support needed to avert sag. This Translite track is made of lightweight aluminum and can be anodized in a variety of colors. Both spots and pendant fixtures are available. The system uses Translite's patented, autofusing power supply.

Electrified Truss/Lucifer Lighting The Electrified Truss system is a miniature system with Lucifer Lighting's track and spotlights fully incorporated in the truss design. The truss operates on a 12-volt circuit, and accepts Lucifer's range of tiny, low-voltage spotlights. Lamp sources are MR 11 and MR 16 quartz halogen lamps. The truss can be suspended or surface mounted, vertically or horizontally, and can be custom angled for projects in retail display, commercial interiors and exhibit booth settings.
photograph by **Tracey Maurer**

Virosa /David D'Imperio The Virosa wall light from David D'Imperio is constructed of chromium-plated brass and nylon, with a yellow, wood shade and aluminum-finished, cast resin base. It uses a 20-watt halogen lamp, and has a transformer with dimmer. The head rotates 180 degrees, and the arm extends a maximum of 24 inches. The base is 10 inches long, 2¼ inches wide and 2 inches high.

Titania/Luceplan USA Titania's elliptical-shaped body of reflecting and screening aluminum-strip construction is offered in a natural or black anodized finish. The supporting cable is nylon, independent from the electrical cable connection, and is adjustable at installation. The ceiling canopy mounts to a standard junction box. The fixture, designed by Alberto Medi and Paolo Rizzatto for Luceplan USA, is supplied with green color filters only, but optional color filters are available. It is lamped with one maximum 250-watt halogen lamp. An optional counterweight is also available.

Spectra/Targetti Sankey S.P.A.
The Spectra series from Targetti Sankey S.P.A. includes wall-mounted and pendant luminaires constructed of metal and glass that feature extraordinary, colored-light effects. The use of glass with special multilayer dichroic treatment allows the coloring of the wall on which the light beam is projected, creating stunning, luminous effects.

ARCHITECTS, LIGHTING AND INTERIOR DESIGNERS

Adams/Mohler Architects
Rik Adams, Rick Mohler
3515 Fremont Avenue North
Seattle, Washington 98103
United States
Tel: (206) 632-2443
Fax: (206) 632-9023

Anthony Belluschi Architects
Anthony Belluschi, Mike Sullivan
55 West Monroe Street
Chicago, Illinois 60603
United States
Tel: (312) 236-6751
Fax: (312) 782-5191

Antunovich Associates
224 West Huron Street, Suite 7 East
Chicago, Illinois 60610
United States
Tel: (312) 266-1126
Fax: (312) 266-7123

Douglas Baker Lighting Consultant
Douglas Baker, IALD
22 Everett Street
Newport, Rhode Island 02840
United States
Tel: (401) 846-9100
Fax: (401) 846-9101

Bass Pro Architecture
1700 South Campbell, Suite L
Springfield, Missouri 65807
United States
Tel: (417) 863-8446
Fax: (417) 863-8082

Tami Bitter
Scalamandre
37-24 24th Street
Long Island City, New York 11101
United States
Tel: (718) 361-8500

Branson Coates Architecture
Doug Branson, Nigel Coates
23 Old Street
London GC1V 9Hl
England
Tel: 44 171 490-0343
Fax: 44 171 490-0320

Byrns, Kendall
& Schieferdecker, Architects
11 West 25th Street
New York, New York 10010
United States
Tel: (212) 807-0127
Fax: (212) 727-9067

Craig A. Roeder Associates, Inc.
Craig A. Roeder, Robert Oakes
3829 North Hall Street
Dallas, Texas 75219
United States
Tel: (214) 528-2300
Fax: (214) 521-2300

Pat Culeto
Culeto Consulting and Design
2350 Marinship Way, #A-001
Sausalito, California 94965
United States
Tel: (415) 331-0880
Fax: (415) 331-2954

Olvia Demetriou
Adamstein & Demetriou Architects
4635 Kenmore Drive, N.W.
Washington, D.C. 20007
United States
Tel: (202) 333-9038
Fax: (202) 337-8830

David Evans
Quinn Evans/Architects
219½ North Main Street
Ann Arbor, Michigan 48104
United States
Tel: (313) 663-5888
Fax: (313) 663-5044

FRCH Design Worldwide
Charles Aenelle, Eugene Allison
Mike Beeghly, Erik Brown
311 Elm Street
Cincinnati, Ohio 45202
United States
Tel: (513) 241-3000
Fax: (513) 241-5015

Celeste Gainey
Gotham Light & Power Company
4433 Campbell Drive
Los Angeles, California 90066
United States
Tel: (310) 390-1318
Fax: (310) 390-1500

Gary Steffy Lighting Design
Gary Steffy, Gary Woodall
2900 South State Street, Suite 12
Ann Arbor, Michigan 48104
United States
Tel: (313) 747-6630
Fax: (313) 747-6629

Russ Halley
Edward Keith Interiors
1047 South Glenstone
Springfield, Missouri 65804
United States
Tel: (417) 866-7251
Fax: (417) 866-6010

Sam Hatch
Hatch Design Group
3198-D Airport Loop Drive
Costa Mesa, California 92626
United States
Tel: (714) 979-8385
Fax: (714) 979-6430

HKS, Inc.
700 North Pearl Street, Suite 1100
Dallas, Texas 75201
United States
Tel: (214) 969-5599
Fax: (214) 969-3397

Motoko Ishii
Motoko Ishii Lighting Design Inc.
Mil Design House 5-4-11, Sendagaya
Shibuya-ku, Tokyo 151
Japan
Tel: 81-3-3353-5311
Fax: 81-3-3353-5120

Chip Israel
Lighting Design Alliance
1234 East Burnett Street
Long Beach, California 90806-3847
United States
Tel: (310) 989-3843
Fax: (310) 989-3847

James Weiner Architect
James Weiner, Peter C. Merwin
1514 17th Street, Studio 207
Santa Monica, California 90404
United States
Tel: (310) 453-5573
Fax: (310) 453-7889

Ann Kale
Ann Kale Associates, Inc.
48 West 25th Street, 12th floor
New York, New York 10010
United States
Tel: (212) 604-0468
Fax: (212) 627-0038

Kume Architects-Engineers
2-1-22, Shiomi
135 Koto-ku, Tokyo
Japan
Tel: 81-3-5632-7811

Barbara Lazaroff
Imaginings
805 Sierra Drive
Beverly Hills, California 90210
United States

Mitsubishi Estate Co., Ltd.
4-1 Marunouchi 2-chome
Chiyoda-ku
Tokyo 100
Japan
Tel: 81-3-3287-5111

Pam Morris
Pam Morris Designs:
Exciting Lighting
14 East Sir Francis Drake Boulevard
Larkspur, California 94939
United States
Tel: (415) 925-0840
Fax: (415) 925-1305

Charles Morris Mount
Charles Morris Mount Inc.
300 West 108th Street
New York, New York 10025
United States
Tel: (212) 864-2937
Fax: (212) 864-0558

Nikken Sekkei Ltd.
2-38, Yokobori, Higashi-ku
Osaka 541
Japan
Tel: 81-6-203-2361

Rambusch Decorating Company
Edwin P. Rambusch,
Martin Rambusch
40 West 13th Street
New York, New York 10011
United States
Tel: (212) 675-0400
Fax: (212) 620-4687

Randy Burkett Lighting Design Inc.
Randy Burkett, Ronald Kurtz
127 Kendrick Plaza, Suite 207
St. Louis, Missouri 63119
United States
Tel: (314) 961-6650
Fax: (314) 961-7640

David Rockwell
Rockwell Group
5 Union Square West
New York, New York 10003
United States
Tel: (212) 463-0334
Fax: (212) 463-0335

Shigeru Uchida
Studio 80
1-17-14 Minami-Aoyama
Minato-Ku, Tokyo 107
Japan
Tel: 81-3-3479-5071
Fax: 81-3-3475-4586

William Rawn Associates, Architects
101 Tremont Street
Boston, Massachusetts 02108
United States
Tel: (617) 423-3470
Fax: (617) 451-9205

Yarnell Associates
  Bruce Yarnell, Derek Porter
12616 West 71st Street
Shawnee, Kansas 66216
United States
Tel: (913) 268-9206
Fax: (913) 268-4468

Gerry Zekowski
Gerry Zekowski Lighting
8256 East Prairie
Skokie, Illinois 60076
United States
Tel: (847) 673-4949

PHOTOGRAPHERS

Peter Aaron
Esto Photographics
222 Valley Place
Mamaroneck, New York 10543
United States
Tel: (914) 698-1033
Fax: (914) 698-4060

Arch Photo/Eduard Hueber
104 Sullivan Street
New York, New York 10012
United States
Tel: (212) 941-9294
Fax: (212) 941-9317

Bass Pro Shops
1700 Campbell Avenue, Suite L
Springfield, Missouri 65807
United States
Tel: (417) 863-8446
Fax: (417) 863-8082

Tom Bonner
1201 Abbot Kinney Boulevard
Venice, California 90291
United States
Tel: (310) 396-7125
Fax: (310) 396-4792

Branson Coates Architecture
  Peter Fleissig, Steve White
23 Old Street
London EC1V 9HL
England
Tel: 44 171 490-0343
Fax: 44 171 490-0320

Cameron Carothers
1340 Glenwood Road, #8
Glendale, California 75219
United States
Tel: (214) 246-1057

Robt Ames Cook
103 Virginia Court
Franklin, Tennessee 37064
United States
Tel: (615) 591-3270
Fax: (615) 591-0937

George Cott
Chroma, Inc.
2802 Azeele Street
Tampa, Florida 33609
United States
Tel: (813) 873-1374
Fax: (813) 871-3448

Delta Queen Steamboat Co.
30 Robin Street Wharf
New Orleans, Louisiana 70130
United States
Tel: (504) 585-0630
Fax: (504) 585-0630

Disney Development Company
200 Celebration Place
Celebration, Florida 34747
United States
Tel: (407) 566-1900
Fax: (407) 566-1999

Martin Fine
10072 Larwin Avenue, #1
Chatsworth, California 91322
United States
Tel: (818) 341-7113

Gnuse/Coker Associates, Inc.
2911 Turtle Creek Boulevard, Suite 300
Dallas, Texas 75219
United States
Tel: (214) 559-4310
Fax: (214) 522-0956

Fred Golden
Golden Photography
1510 Franklin Street
Ann Arbor, Michigan 48103
United States
Tel: (313) 663-2040

Hiroyuki Hirai
Hiroyuki Hirai Shashin Jimusho
23-7-201 Maruyama-Cho
Shibuya-Ku, Tokyo 150
Japan
Tel: 81-3-3462-5504

Yutaka Kohno
Motoko Ishii Lighting Design Inc.
Mil Design House 5-4-11, Sendagaya
Shibuya-ku, Tokyo 151
Japan
Tel: 81-3-3353-5311
Fax: 81-3-3353-5120

Maxwell Mackenzie
2641 Garfield Street, N.W.
Washington, D.C. 20008
United States
Tel: (202) 232-6686
Fax: (202) 232-6684

Akihisa Masuda
Motoko Ishii Lighting Design Inc.
Mil Design House 5-4-11, Sendagaya
Shibuya-ku, Tokyo 151
Japan
Tel: 81-3-3353-5311
Fax: 81-3-3353-5120

Norman McGrath
164 West 79th Street
New York, New York 10024
United States
Tel: (212) 799-6422
Fax: (212) 799-1285

Jon Miller
Hedrich-Blessing
11 West Illinois Street
Chicago, Illinois 60610
United States
Tel: (312) 321-1151
Fax: (312) 321-1165

James R. Morse
208 East 28th Street, Box 26
New York, New York 10016
United States
Tel: (212) 889-1550

Robert Pisano
7527 15th Avenue, N.E.
Seattle, Washington 98115
United States
Tel: (206) 525-3500
Fax: (206) 525-2234

Stan Ries
Stan Ries Photography
48 Great Jones Street
New York, New York 10012
United States
Tel: (212) 533-1852
Fax: (212) 533-1852

Steve Rosenthal
Steve Rosenthal Photography
59 Maple Street
Auburndale, Massachusetts 02166
United States
Tel: (617) 244-2986
Fax: (617) 244-9824

Bill Rothschild
19 Judith Lane
Monsey, New York 10952
United States
Tel: (212) 752-3674

Paul Warchol
Paul Warchol Photography
133 Mulberry Street
New York, New York 10013
United States
Tel: (212) 431-3461
Fax: (212) 274-1953

Christopher Wesnofske
280 Park Avenue South, #16C
New York, New York 10010
United States
Tel: (212) 473-0993

Kenneth Wyner
7012 Westmoreland Avenue
Tacoma Park, Maryland 20912
United States
Tel: (301) 495-9475

Yoichi Yamazaki
Motoko Ishii Lighting Design Inc.
Mil Design House 5-4-11, Sendagaya
Shibuya-ku, Tokyo 151
Japan
Tel: 81-3-3353-5311
Fax: 81-3-3353-5120

LIGHTING MANUFACTURERS

Adesso Lighting
21 Penn Plaza, Suite 1001
New York, New York 10019
United States
Tel: (212) 736-4440
Fax: (212) 736-4806

Artemide Inc.
1980 New Highway
Farmingdale, New York 11735
United States
Tel: (516) 694-9292
Fax: (516) 694-9275

Azizi
P.O. Box 7761
Newport Beach, California 92660
United States
Tel: (714) 645-6332

Baldinger Architectural Lighting Inc.
19-02 Steinway Street
Astoria, New York 11105
United States
Tel: (718) 204-5700
Fax: (718) 721-4986

David Bergman Architects
245 Eldridge Street
New York, New York 10002
United States
Tel: (212) 475-3106
Fax: (212) 677-7291

Boyd Lighting Company
56 12th Street
San Francisco, California 94103
United States
Tel: (415) 778-4300
Fax: (415) 778-4319

Casella Lighting
111 Rhode Island Street
San Francisco, California 94103
United States
Tel: (415) 626-9600
Fax: (415) 626-4539

Cini & Nils
Via Francesco Ferruccio 8
20145 Milano
Italy
Tel: 02-3495088

David D'Imperio
2961 Aviation Avenue
Miami, Florida 33133
United States
Tel: (305) 285-1298
Fax: (305) 285-1130

Expo Design
1 Elm Street
Locust Valley, New York 11560
United States
Tel: (516) 674-1420
Fax: (516) 674-6778

Face Lights
60 Clementina Street
San Francisco, California 94105
United States
Tel: (415) 957-8719
Fax: (415) 957-1380

Flos Incorporated
200 McKay Road
Huntington Station, New York 11746
United States
Tel: (516) 549-2745
Fax: (516) 549-4220

Ingo Maurer GmbH
Kaiserstrasse 47
D-80801 Munich
Germany
Tel: 089-381606-0

Interfold
P.O. Box 3396
Santa Rosa, California 95402
United States
Tel: (707) 526-5619

Justice Design Group Inc.
3457 South La Cienega Boulevard
Los Angeles, California 90016
United States
Tel: (310) 836-9575
Fax: (310) 397-7170

Kane Shrader Custom Designs
898 Production Place
Newport Beach, California 92663
United States
Tel: (714) 548-2131

Lam Lighting Systems
2200 South Anne Street
Santa Ana, California 92704-4484
United States
Tel: (714) 549-9765
Fax: (714) 662-4515

Lamps By Hilliard
886 A Street
Arcata, California 95521
United States
Tel: (707) 826-1545
Fax: (707) 826-1561

Le Collezioni
Merchandise Mart, 1498
World Trade Center
Chicago, Illinois 60654
United States

Lightolier
100 Lighting Way
Secaucus, New Jersey 07096
United States
Tel: (201) 864-3000

Luceplan USA
315 Hudson Street
New York, New York 10013
United States
Tel: (212) 989-6265
Fax: (212) 462-4349

Lucifer Lighting Company
414 Live Oak Street
San Antonio, Texas 78202
United States
Tel: 1-800-879-9797

Manning Lighting
1810 North Avenue
Sheboygan, Wisconsin 53082
United States
Tel: (414) 458-2184
Fax: (414) 458-2491

Metalum
340 East Shore Road
Jamestown, Rhode Island 02835
United States
Tel: (401) 423-3788

Meyda Tiffany
55 Oriskany Boulevard
Yorkville, New York 13495
United States
Tel: (315) 768-3711

New Metal Crafts
812 North Wells Street
Chicago, Illinois 60610
United States
Tel: (312) 787-6991
Fax: (312) 787-8692

Optelma AG
Gartenstrasse 7
CH-4537 Wiedlisbach
Switzerland
Tel: 065/763033

R/D Design
2625 Alcatraz Avenue, #149
Berkeley, California 94705
United States
Tel: (510) 451-5800

SPI Lighting Inc.
10400 North Enterprise Drive
Mequon, Wisconsin 53092
United States
Tel: (414) 242-1420
Fax: (414) 242-6414

Targetti Sankey S.P.A.
Via Pratese 164
50145 Firenze
Italy
Tel: 055-3791.1

Tech Lighting, Inc.
2542 North Elston
Chicago, Illinois 60647
United States
Tel: (312) 252-0008
Fax: (312) 252-4264

Translite, Inc.
120 Wampus Lane
Milford, Connecticut 06460
United States
Tel: (203) 878-8567

Visa Lighting
8600 West Bradley Road
Milwaukee, Wisconsin 53224
United States
Tel: (414) 354-6600

Yamagiwa Corporation Tokyo
101 4-1-1 Sotokanda
Chiyodaku, Tokyo
Japan
Tel: 03-3253-2111

Z-Axis, Inc.
P.O. Box 2087
Boone, North Carolina 28607
United States
Tel: (704) 963-8797

INDEX

ACKNOWLEDGMENTS

My gratitude and appreciation go to all the designers and photographers who contributed their fine work to this book. My special thanks is offered to Howard Brandston and Viggo Bech Rambusch, whose words have made this book not only very special for its readers, but for its author as well.

I have been working with PBC International Inc. for ten years now on design books and would like to take this opportunity to thank everyone on staff there for their professionalism and patience. It has been an honor for me to have my name on some of the beautiful and high-quality books they publish. Specifically regarding this book, kudos go to Susan Kapsis, Managing Editor; Jennifer Moglia, Editorial Assistant; Richard Liu, Technical Director; and Maria Corio, the Artist who designed this book. Thanks, PBC, for enriching my career as well as enriching the "design souls" of all who read your books!